An INDIAN FAMILY *recipe book*

LAXMI KHURANA

ROBINSON

ROBINSON

First published in Great Britain in 1985 by Elliot Right Way Books

This edition published in Great Britain in 2022 by Robinson

1 3 5 7 9 10 8 6 4 2

A CIP catalogue record for this book
is available from the British Library.

ISBN 978-1-47214-698-4

Typeset by Peran Publishing Services
Printed and bound in Great Britain by Clays Ltd, Elcograf S.p.A.

Papers used by Robinson are from well-managed forests
and other responsible sources

Robinson
An imprint of
Little, Brown Book Group
Carmelite House
50 Victoria Embankment
London EC4Y 0DZ

An Hachette UK Company
www.hachette.co.uk

www.littlebrown.co.uk

NOTE: The material contained in this book is set out in good faith for general
guidance and no liability can be accepted for loss or expense incurred as a result of
relying in particular circumstances on statements made in the book. Laws and
regulations are complex and liable to change, and readers should check the
current position with relevant authorities before making personal arrangements.

How To Books are published by Robinson, an imprint of Little, Brown Book Group. We
welcome proposals from authors who have first-hand experience of their subjects. Please
set out the aims of your book, its target market and its suggested contents in an email to
HowTo@littlebrown.co.uk

PREFACE

The author is an Indian housewife, living in Britain. She enjoys cooking and has made it one of her particular hobbies and interests. When entertaining friends she has often heard remarks to the effect that Indian cooking is complicated, time-consuming and very difficult. This is not true. Indian cooking can be fun and simple. This book removes the myths, and explains Indian cooking by straightforward step by step methods. Many of the recipes in the book are for 'family' dishes which would not be served in restaurants. Hence the title *An Indian Family Recipe Book*.

ACKNOWLEDGEMENTS

Writing a book while in full time employment is not easy. My family and especially my children have shown a lot of patience and given me every encouragement. My children and many of my friends have been guinea pigs for testing the recipes. I would therefore like to thank all my friends for their efforts, and the question – Why don't you write a book? This is basically what started it.

So I would like to dedicate the book to my two children Micky and Reeta and my husband, without whose efforts this book would have never seen completion.

CONTENTS

INTRODUCTION

Indian food, and spicy food in general, has become common and increasingly popular outside India over the past few decades. This is especially true in the UK, where cosmopolitan influences have increased the number of non-English restaurants considerably. In spite of all this, there remains a myth that Indian cooking is cumbersome and time-consuming. This book explains how Indian cooking can be simple, based on a few, well-known spices which are easily available.

For simplicity I have divided Indian cooking into a number of sections: starters; savoury snacks; meat and fish curries; dhals; vegetable curries; chutneys, pickles and raitas; sundries, like chapattis, rice, etc; and sweets. Starters and meat curry dishes are pretty standard, and easily understood by most people. However, the dhals and vegetable curries offer a lot of variety and are much used in Indian homes, but are not so readily available in restaurants. Therefore, besides covering the more popular meat and sundry cookery, this book covers a range of dhal and vegetable dishes to give you the opportunity of trying them.

Utensils and Equipment
Here are some basic utensils and equipment needed for Indian cooking:
- a tava – heavy-based flat pan which can be bought at most Indian shops. If this is not available, then a large heavy-based frying pan can be used;
- a liquidizer or food processor;
- a sieve or skimmer (used for deep frying foods);
- a wok, or a large, deep frying pan;
- a colander; and
- a large serving spoon (marked with spoon measurements).

In India, and in many restaurants in the UK, a tandoor is often used. The tandoor is a clay oven, which is heated to a very high temperature in excess of 800°F (430°C). Most Indian homes in the UK do not have a tandoor, and therefore normally use an ordinary oven for tandoori dishes.

Ingredients

Some of the commonly used ingredients include: tandoori masala, garam masala, madras curry powder, garlic, ginger (both fresh and powdered), chilli powder, turmeric powder, hing (asafoetida), coriander (fresh, seeds and powdered), black peppercorns, cinnamon, cardamom, cloves, nutmeg, cumin (both seeds and powdered), fennel seeds, fenugreek seeds, rai (both black mustard seeds and powder), soy sauce and ghee.

Tandoori masala, garam masala and madras curry powder are mixtures of other spices.

Tandoori masala is a combination of salt, coriander, cardamom powder, cinnamon powder, black peppercorns, cumin powder, ground cloves, chilli powder, ground bay leaves, mace, nutmeg, fenugreek powder, garlic powder and ginger powder. It is easily available in most large supermarkets.

Garam masala is a combination of coriander powder, cumin powder, black peppercorns, ginger powder, cinnamon powder, pimento, cardamom powder, ground bay leaves, ground cloves and nutmeg. This again is easily available in large supermarkets.

Madras curry powder, again very easily available from most supermarkets, is a mixture of cumin powder, chillies, turmeric powder, ground mustard seeds, ground poppy seeds, garlic powder, and ground fenugreek.

Ginger is available in both fresh and powder form, and is a reddish-brown coloured root. To use fresh ginger, remove the skin of the root and then chop finely. In powdered form, the root is first dried and then ground. Ginger can be purchased already powdered.

Garlic, again, is available in both fresh and powdered form. It is a very strong-smelling bulb, consisting of a number of small sections, known as cloves of garlic. To use fresh garlic, remove the skin from the clove, and chop finely. For the powdered form, the garlic is dried and then ground, or it can be purchased already powdered.

Chilli powder is often available in varying degrees of hotness. I recommend that milder forms of chilli powder are used initially. After some time, when you really want to try extra hot dishes, then either use slightly larger quantities of mild chilli powder, or buy a hotter variety.

Fresh green chillies are used in many recipes. If these are chopped by hand (rather than a liquidizer or food processor), you should make sure that you wash your hands with soap immediately after cutting them. This is essential because otherwise a burning sensation will be felt on your hands. This sensation transfers to any other part of your body that you touch. Fresh green chillies are available at most supermarkets.

Turmeric powder is the powdered form of the stem of a plant. It is bright yellow in colour and is widely available.

Hing (asafoetida) is a gum resin which is available either in gum or powder form. It has a very strong smell, and is mainly used for flavouring. It also aids digestion. It is available in most Indian shops but is not generally found in supermarkets. Some of the curries in this book use hing, but if it is not available, then the curry can be cooked without it. The fragrance of the curry will be less strong but only a small difference in taste is apparent.

Coriander is available in three forms: fresh, which is a green leaf used for garnishing and flavouring; powder, which is used for flavouring; and seeds, which are sometimes used for growing fresh coriander. Powdered coriander is easily available, but fresh coriander can be difficult to obtain. If it is not available then use fresh parsley for garnishing instead.

Black peppercorns are mainly used in savoury snacks and biryanis. It is the fruit of a plant and is easily obtainable in most supermarkets. Powdered form is often used in raitas and pickles.

Cinnamon is also available in two forms: cinnamon stick, which is the dried bark of the Asiatic shrub, broken into smaller pieces; and the powdered form, which can be used instead of the stick. The powdered form can be easily obtained.

Cardamom is a dried fruit with very aromatic seeds. Several of the seeds are enclosed together in a light green or creamish-white coloured pod. The pod can be used whole, or the seeds can be removed from the pods and then used.

Cloves are the dried flower buds of a special Asiatic tree. They are used whole, for flavouring, in many curries.

Nutmeg is the very hard, aromatic seed of a tree. The seeds are ground, and powdered nutmeg is easily available in most supermarkets.

Cumin is the dried fruit of an umbrella type of plant (umbelliferous), which is used for flavouring. Both the powdered form and the seeds are very widely used in curries and pickles. Both forms are easily available from supermarkets.

Fennel seeds, like cumin, are also a dried fruit. They are used in some recipes and for making tea. Fennel seeds, light green in colour, have a very mild bitter taste. They are also often eaten raw.

Fenugreek seeds are very dark orange in colour and are often used to grow fresh fenugreek. Ground fenugreek is used in making various mixed spices and in chutneys and pickles. Fresh fenugreek is a vegetable, sometimes cooked like spinach.

Rai (black mustard seeds) are the seeds from the pods of yellow flowers of a small plant. The seeds are used for flavouring curries, and the powdered form is used for pickles. Both varieties of rai are available from most Asian shops or large supermarkets. Sometimes health food shops also sell rai.

Soy sauce, an extract of soya beans, is not commonly used in India. Elsewhere, however, many Indian homes use it for cooking curries.

Ghee can be obtained from some Indian shops, but clarified butter could be used in its place. Clarified butter can be made by boiling unsalted butter itself for about 20 minutes, allowing it to cool, and then skimming off the scum on the surface to leave a clear liquid. If salted butter is used, then the clear liquid should be poured off, and the salt residue left in the pan. The clear liquid solidifies after cooling and is used for cooking. The residue is thrown away.

Most of these spices can be obtained in bulk, and stored in a cool place for up to nine months or a year. It is a lot cheaper to buy spices in this way than to buy an occasional two or four ounce packet. If you find it difficult to obtain garam masala, tandoori masala, madras curry powder or any of the other spices, there are a number of Indian shops which sell by post.

Marinating

In Indian cooking, the process of marinating is frequently used to flavour foods. Marinating is often done by soaking the food to be flavoured in a mixture of yoghurt and spices. The minimum amount of time for marinating is about four hours, but the longer you leave food marinating, the better it tastes. This is especially true of tandoori dishes, where the fresh meat needs to marinate for about eight to twelve hours. Marination also serves to tenderise meat.

Dhals

Dhals, often called pulses, are different types of seeds, used to make a variety of dishes. There are about fifteen different types of dhals; and again these can be bought in bulk and stored for up to a year. It is very difficult to describe all the different types of seeds in English; only a couple are well-known in English households, namely lentils and chickpeas. Most other varieties are available in Indian shops, and the Indian names may be used to buy them. Dhals are an acquired taste, and there is a tremendous variety in the way they can be cooked and, accordingly, in their flavour. They are usually served with rice, or another curry. Care must be taken in cooking dhals, to ensure that the seeds are well-boiled. They should not be eaten raw. This is because, unless cooked properly, they can be difficult to digest. In all the dhal recipes, cooking times should be carefully adhered to.

Different types of dhals are often ground to make flour. This flour is used to make poppadums, dhokra and a variety of other dishes. Also used in Indian cooking are two very commonly used flours: besan, or gram, flour, and chapatti flour. Besan flour is made from ground black grams, which are pulses. Chapatti flour is made from ground wheat. Neither of these flours has a direct English equivalent, but are easily obtainable from Indian shops, or health food stores.

Dhals often contain impurities like dust particles and chaff. So before they are cooked, they need to be washed properly. This is done in one of the following two ways:

- The seeds can be individually sorted out, a few at a time and the impurities individually picked out. This method is the best, but is very laborious and time-consuming.
- A faster method which is nearly as successful is to wash the dhal in such a way that the impurities sink to the bottom or float to the top. This is done by taking two large pans and placing the dhal in one of them. Add plenty of cold water so that it covers the dhal by about two inches. Now shake the pan so as to stir the dhal. The chaff floats to the top and can be thrown away. Transfer the rest of the contents gradually to the second pan

until very little dhal is left in the first pan. The impurities should be at the bottom with this small amount of dhal. This residue can either be discarded with the impurities or carefully picked so that all the impurities are thrown away. Repeat this process of mixing fresh water, stirring and transferring the contents back and forth about six to seven times. This method has something in common with the principles of 'gold panning' in olden times.

Vegetables
There is a tremendous variety of vegetable dishes in Indian cooking. Most of the vegetables are sold in English shops, e.g. potatoes, peas, aubergines, okra and peppers. The book does, however, include recipes which contain four rather uncommon vegetables. These are tindora, vallour, kadu and guaer. These are available from most Indian shops, and obviously have to be bought fresh. The closest approximation to any one of these four special vegetables is marrow, which can be used instead of kadu.

These uncommon dishes are well worth a try if you enjoy experimenting and are vegetarian. The Indian names can be used to buy these vegetables.

Raitas
Raitas are made from fresh natural yoghurt. Most Indian households make their own natural yoghurt, and raitas always taste better with freshly made yoghurt. Obviously they are not a main meal, but could be described as sundry dishes.

Pickles and Chutneys
Pickles and chutneys are always available at the table – in fact, an Indian meal would be incomplete without a variety of them. You can buy many ready-made pickles from most English supermarkets, or else prepare your own, as shown in some of the recipes.

Quantities of Ingredients

Indian cooking is an acquired art. You can never be very precise about the quantity of spices; it depends very much on your own taste. Sometimes it is worth experimenting with quantities until you arrive at the blend which suits your own taste buds. It is always best to start with a minimum of spices, as I do in this book. After a while, perhaps you might like to add other spices to the recipes in very small quantities, to experiment with flavours. You should not be afraid to do this, as all Indian cooking has been handed down through the generations, each generation varying the blends of spices in its own way.

In most Indian households today, the same curry cooked on different days may well taste slightly different. The measurements of spices in this book should therefore be used more as basic guidelines, rather than as hard and fast rules.

Since this book is mainly aimed at the reader who is cooking for a family, I have constructed most of the recipes as enough to feed four people. If the dining table is to be shared by a larger or by a smaller number, then the amount of each ingredient must be increased, or reduced, proportionately.

Some ingredients like bay leaves and cloves are used for cooking but not eaten. The curry is served with these ingredients left in, but the person eating discards them at the side of the plate.

Preparation and Cooking Times

For convenience I have included a preparation and cooking time for each recipe. This is the total period from the moment of beginning work on the recipe until the time the food is to be served. Some of these times are quite long – several hours in a few instances. Of course this does not mean that the housewife is busy for hours just to make the one meal! The preparation and cooking times include the periods during which the ingredients are soaking or marinating

– an important procedure which imparts the characteristic flavour to many Indian recipes. But these times do indicate to the busy housewife whether a particular recipe can be ready for supper tonight!

Serving the meal
As a final note, you may be interested to know how a typical Indian meal would be served. Usually it would start with drinks, and an assortment of savoury snacks, while sitting around before dinner. Once at the table, the meal typically begins with a starter, and this is followed by one or two meat dishes, accompanied by a rice dish with one vegetable curry and/or dhal. Chapattis or parothas or puris are also served at the same time, but usually only one of the options is served. Raitas, poppadums and a variety of pickles and chutneys should also be placed on the table, together with a fresh salad. Normally, as the dishes are laid out, the diners help themselves to a selection of each as they require.

Drinks to accompany Indian meals are usually non-alcoholic, as the spicy food tends to detract from the flavour of wine, and vice versa. Therefore, either iced water with a slice of lemon and a small amount of sugar is served, or lassi (yoghurt and water combined). However, wine or beer can be served, according to individual taste.

Once the main course is finished, the sweet is served, followed by coffee or tea. Indian tea is made by adding tea, a teaspoonful of fennel seeds and 2 or 3 cardamoms to water, bringing the water to the boil and boiling for about 3 to 4 minutes, adding milk and boiling again for about 2 to 3 minutes, thus making a strong brew of tea. This is usually served, accompanied by fennel seeds mixed with sugar crystals, on a plate.

This should give you some guidelines, if you are planning on having a full Indian meal, on how to serve, and what dishes to combine.

1
STARTERS

ONION BHAJIS
(Onion Rings fried in gram flour batter)

Serves 4.

Preparation and cooking time: 40 mins.

This is one of the many Indian starter dishes. It can also be used as a snack served with a glass of wine, etc. For this recipe you will need a liquidizer and a deep frying pan or wok.

10g ($^1/_2$oz) fresh ginger, peeled
10g ($^1/_2$oz) fresh garlic, peeled
4 green chillies
85g (3oz) besan flour (gram flour)
$^1/_2$ tsp salt
$^1/_2$ tsp chilli powder
$^1/_2$ tsp garam masala
$^1/_2$ tsp tandoori masala
90ml (3fl oz) water
2 largish onions, cut into rings
600ml (20fl oz) cooking oil for deep frying

Method

1. Put the ginger, garlic and green chillies into a liquidizer and process until very finely chopped.
2. Sieve the gram flour into a mixing bowl. Add the contents of the liquidizer, salt, chilli powder, garam masala, tandoori masala and mix well. Add the water and mix well again into a thickish, smooth batter.
3. Add the onion rings to the batter and mix gently so that the onions are well covered with batter.
4. Heat the oil to a high temperature in a small wok, or deep frying pan. When the oil is hot, remove the onion rings one at a time from the batter and deep fry in the oil. This method of frying onions is similar to frying chips or fish in batter. Fry only 6 to 7 rings at a time.
5. Serve the onion bhajis while they are still hot.

POTATO PAKORAS

(Thinly sliced potatoes in gram flour batter)

Serves 4.

Preparation and cooking time: 30 mins.

This is another savoury snack which can be served at high teas. It is also a good starter to a main meal. Potato lovers will enjoy this dish. Most children are very fond of potato pakoras. For this recipe you need a deep frying pan or wok.

170g (6oz) besan flour (gram flour)
120ml (4fl oz) water
340g (12oz) potatoes, peeled and sliced finely, similar to crisps, but slightly thicker
$^3/_4$ tsp garlic powder
$^3/_4$ tsp salt
$^3/_4$ tsp chilli powder
$^3/_4$ tsp garam masala
$^3/_4$ tsp turmeric powder
600ml (20fl oz) cooking oil for frying

Method
1. Sieve the gram flour into a mixing bowl.
2. Mix the flour, water, potatoes, garlic powder, salt, chilli powder, garam masala, and turmeric powder well.
3. Heat the cooking oil to a high temperature in a wok or deep frying pan. Pick each potato piece individually from the mixture and place it in the hot oil until you have about 10 pieces. The pakoras will float in the oil, and each side should be deep fried until it is golden orange. With a sieve, drain the pakoras.
4. Repeat with the remaining pakoras and serve while hot.

SPINACH PAKORAS

(Sliced spinach in gram flour batter)

Serves 4.

Preparation and cooking time: 30 mins.

This is another savoury snack which can be served at high teas. It is also a good starter to a main meal. Spinach lovers will really enjoy spinach pakoras. For this recipe you need a deep frying pan or wok.

110g (4oz) besan flour (gram flour)
55g (2oz) spinach, finely chopped
90ml (3fl oz) water
$^3/_4$ tsp salt
$^3/_4$ tsp chilli powder
3 green chillies, finely chopped
$^3/_4$ tsp turmeric powder
600ml (20fl oz) cooking oil for frying

Method
1. Sieve the gram flour into a mixing bowl.
2. Mix the flour, spinach, water, salt, chilli powder, chillies and turmeric powder well.
3. Heat cooking oil to a high temperature in a wok or deep frying pan. Take a teaspoonful of the spinach mixture and place it gently in the hot oil. Repeat this until you have about 10 pieces. After a few seconds the pieces will float to the top of the oil. Then fry each side of the spinach pakora until it is golden orange. This frying process should take about 4 to 5 minutes, otherwise the oil is too hot and therefore the heat should be lowered. With a sieve, drain the pakoras and place them on kitchen roll paper.
4. Repeat with the remaining spinach mixture.
5. Transfer the pakoras to a serving dish and serve while hot.

MIXED PAKORAS

(Onions, potatoes and spinach in gram flour batter)

Serves 4.

Preparation and cooking time: 40 mins.

This is another savoury dish which can be used as a starter or a snack. It can also be served with high teas or at parties. For this recipe you will need a liquidizer or blender and a deep frying pan or wok.

10g ($^1/_2$oz) fresh garlic, peeled
10g ($^1/_2$oz) fresh ginger, peeled
5 green chillies
170g (6oz) besan flour (gram flour)
2 potatoes, peeled and finely chopped
85g (3oz) fresh spinach, finely chopped
1 large onion, finely chopped
1 tsp chilli powder
1 tsp tandoori masala
1 tsp garam masala
1 tsp salt
1 tsp turmeric powder
120ml (4fl oz) water
600ml (20fl oz) cooking oil for frying

Method

1. Put the garlic, ginger and green chillies into a liquidizer and chop finely.

2. Sieve the gram flour into a mixing bowl and mix in the contents of the liquidizer, potatoes, spinach, onion, chilli powder, tandoori masala, garam masala, salt, turmeric powder and water. Mix everything well.

3. Heat the oil to a high temperature in a wok or deep frying pan. Add about 10 tablespoonfuls of the mixture, a tablespoonful at a time, to the heated oil. These will float and should be deep fried for about 3 to 4 minutes, until each of the fried pakoras is golden brown.

4. Remove the pakoras with a sieve and drain the excess oil off them by placing the pakoras on kitchen roll paper.

5. Repeat with the remaining pakoras and serve while hot.

CHICKEN PAKORAS
(Chicken pieces in gram flour batter)

Serves 4.

Preparation and cooking time: 1 hr.

This is another savoury snack which can be served at high teas, parties or even picnics. For this recipe you need a deep frying pan or wok.

450g (1lb) frozen chicken pieces, thawed
110g (4oz) besan flour (gram flour)
120ml (4fl oz) water
$^1/_2$ tsp salt
$^1/_2$ tsp chilli powder
$^1/_2$ tsp garam masala
$^1/_2$ tsp turmeric powder
2 tsp soy sauce
600ml (20fl oz) cooking oil for frying

Method

1. Remove the skin of the chicken pieces and cut the flesh from the bones. Cut the flesh into about 2cm (1 inch) cubes.

2. Bake these chicken cubes in a preheated oven at a temperature of mark 4 (350°F or 180°C) for about 20 minutes. Remove the pieces from the oven and allow them to cool.

3. Sieve the gram flour into a mixing bowl.

4. Mix the flour, water, salt, chilli powder, garam masala, turmeric powder, and soy sauce well to form a thickish paste.

5. Heat the cooking oil to a high temperature in a wok or deep frying pan. Dip each chicken piece individually in the paste and place it in the hot oil until you have about 5 pieces. After a few seconds the chicken pakoras will float to the top of the oil. Deep fry each side of the pakora until it is golden orange. This will usually take about 2 minutes for each side. With a sieve, drain the pakoras.

6. Repeat with the remaining chicken pieces and serve while hot.

FISH PAKORAS
(Fish pieces in gram flour batter)

Serves 4.

Preparation and cooking time: 1 hr.

This is another savoury snack which can be served at high teas, parties or even picnics. It could also be served with chips, instead of the traditional English fish and chips. For this recipe you need a deep frying pan or wok.

450g (1lb) cod fillets
110g (4oz) besan flour (gram flour)
120ml (4fl oz) water
$^1/_2$ tsp salt
$^1/_2$ tsp chilli powder
$^1/_2$ tsp garam masala
$^1/_2$ tsp turmeric powder
2 tsp soy sauce
600ml (20fl oz) cooking oil for frying

Method

1. Cut the fillets into about 5cm (2 inches) long and about 1cm ($^1/_2$ inch) wide pieces.
2. Sieve the gram flour into a mixing bowl.
3. Mix the flour, water, salt, chilli powder, garam masala, turmeric powder, and soy sauce well to form a thickish paste.
4. Heat the cooking oil to a high temperature in a wok or deep frying pan. Lower the heat and leave it for a further 3 to 4 minutes. Dip each fish piece individually in the paste and place it in the hot oil until you have about 5 pieces. After a few seconds the fish pakoras will float to the top of the oil. Deep fry each side of the pakora until it is golden orange. This will usually take about 4 minutes for each side. With a sieve, drain the fish pakoras.
5. Repeat with the remaining fish pieces and serve while hot.

VEGETABLE SAMOSAS

(Indian vegetable pasties)

Makes about 16 samosas.

Preparation and cooking time: 1 hr 20 mins.

This is a savoury snack served at parties or with high teas. It is useful for picnics too, because samosas are tasty even when cold. Raw filled samosas can be stored in a freezer and then fried when needed. For this recipe you need a flat frying pan or tava, and a deep frying pan or wok.

For filling
450g (1lb) potatoes
60ml (2fl oz) cooking oil
$^1/_2$ tsp whole jeera (cumin seeds)
$^1/_2$ tsp whole rai (black mustard seeds)
1 large onion, finely chopped
110g (4oz) frozen peas
1 tsp salt
$^1/_2$ tsp chilli powder
$^1/_2$ tsp tandoori masala
$^1/_2$ tsp turmeric powder
$^1/_2$ tsp garam masala
15ml ($^1/_2$fl oz) lemon juice

For pastry
120ml (4fl oz) water
225g (8oz) plain flour
15ml ($^1/_2$fl oz) lemon juice
A pinch of salt
55g (2oz) plain flour for rolling pastry

For paste
25g (1oz) plain flour
90ml (3fl oz) water
600ml (20fl oz) cooking oil for frying

Method

1. Peel the potatoes and then boil them for about 10 minutes.
2. Cut the boiled potatoes into very small pieces.
3. Heat the 60ml (2fl oz) of oil in a frying pan, and add the jeera, rai, and chopped onion. Cook until the onion is golden brown. Add the potatoes, peas, salt, chilli powder, tandoori masala, turmeric powder, garam masala and lemon juice. Mix all the ingredients well, cook for about 2 minutes and remove the contents from the heat.
4. Mix the 120ml (4fl oz) of water, the 225g (8oz) of plain flour, the 15ml (1/2fl oz) of lemon juice and the pinch of salt into a medium soft dough.
5. Heat a 'tava', or a large flat frying pan, to a high temperature.
6. Divide the dough into 8 roughly equal parts and shape them into round balls. Sprinkle a little bit of the plain flour on to each ball. Roll each ball out flat (like a chapatti), 20cm (about 7 to 8 inches) in diameter. Cook each side on the 'tava' for about 4 seconds.
7. Cut all the cooked chapattis into halves. Now mix the 25g (1oz) of plain flour and the 60ml (2fl oz) of water thoroughly, until the mixture is like glue.
8. Take each half of the rolled chapatti, and form a cone by bringing its two corners together and joining the straight sides together with the paste. Now fill each of the cones with about 2 to 3 tablespoonfuls of the potato mixture and paste together the round ends of the cone. These filled cones are called samosas. Repeat with all the remaining chapattis.
9. These samosas can now be stored in a freezer for a period of up to 6 weeks. If stored in a freezer, they must be thawed for about 1 hour before deep frying.
10. Heat the 600ml (20fl oz) of oil in a wok or a large pan, and deep fry all the samosas, 4 to 5 at a time, until they are golden brown.
11. Serve the samosas hot, with tomato ketchup.

BEEF SAMOSAS

(Indian beef pasties)

Makes about 16 samosas.

Preparation and cooking time: 1 hr 30 mins.

This is a savoury snack served at parties or with high teas. Like vegetable samosas it is useful for picnics. Raw filled samosas can be stored in a freezer and then fried when needed. For this recipe you need a flat frying pan or tava and a deep frying pan or wok.

For filling
30ml (1fl oz) cooking oil
$^1/_2$ tsp whole rai (black mustard seeds)
$^1/_2$ tsp whole jeera (cumin seeds)
1 small onion, finely chopped
8oz (225g) minced beef
55g (2oz) finely chopped potatoes
55g (2oz) finely chopped fresh carrots
$^1/_2$ tsp salt
1 tsp turmeric powder
1 tsp chilli powder
30ml (1fl oz) lemon juice

For pastry
120ml (4fl oz) water
225g (8oz) plain flour
15ml ($^1/_2$fl oz) lemon juice
A pinch of salt
55g (2oz) plain flour for rolling

For paste
25g (1oz) plain flour
60ml (2fl oz) water
600ml (20fl oz) cooking oil for frying

Method

1. Heat the 30ml (1fl oz) of oil in a frying pan to a high temperature, and add the rai, jeera, and the chopped onion. Cook until the onion is golden brown. Add the mince, potatoes, carrots, salt, turmeric powder and chilli powder. Mix all the ingredients well, lower the heat and cover the pan. Simmer the mixture for about 20 minutes stirring every 10 minutes. Now add the 30ml (1fl oz) of lemon juice, switch off the heat and leave the contents to cool.

2. Mix the 60ml (4fl oz) of water, the 225g (8oz) of plain flour, the 15ml (1/2fl oz) of lemon juice and the pinch of salt into a medium soft dough.

3. Heat a 'tava' or a large flat frying pan to a high temperature.

4. Divide the dough into 8 roughly equal parts and shape them into round balls. Sprinkle a little bit of the plain flour on to each of the balls. Roll out each ball flat (like a chapatti), 20cm (about 7 to 8 inches) in diameter. Cook each side on the 'tava' for about 4 seconds.

5. Cut all the cooked chapattis into halves.

6. Now mix the 25g (1oz) of plain flour and the 60ml (2fl oz) of water thoroughly, until the mixture is like glue.

7. Take each half of the rolled chapatti, and form a cone by bringing its two corners together and joining the straight sides together with the paste. Now fill each of the cones with about 2 to 3 tablespoonfuls of the beef mixture and paste together the round ends of the cone. These filled cones are called samosas. Repeat with all the remaining chapattis.

8. These samosas can now be stored in a freezer for a period of up to 6 weeks. If stored in a freezer, they must be thawed for about 1 hour before deep frying.

9. Heat the 600ml (20fl oz) of oil in a wok or a large pan, and deep fry all the samosas, 4 to 5 at a time, until they are golden brown.

10. Serve the samosas hot, with tomato ketchup.

TANDOORI SPARE RIB PORK CHOPS WITH SALAD

Serves 4.

Preparation and cooking time: 5 hrs 30 mins.

This is usually served as a mild starter. It can be used as a main dish, served with pilaw rice. During summer days, it makes an excellent addition to salad, instead of ham or cold chicken. For this recipe you can either buy small (about 7.5cm/3 inch long) pork chops or get your butcher to cut large chops into halves. You will require a liquidizer for this recipe.

90ml (3fl oz) plain yoghurt
1 tsp salt
1 tsp turmeric powder
2 tsp tomato purée
2 tsp tandoori masala
55g (2oz) fresh garlic, peeled
$^{1}/_{2}$ tsp chilli powder
55g (2oz) fresh ginger, peeled
4 green chillies
5–6 drops red food colouring
900g (2lb) small spare rib pork chops
60ml (2fl oz) cooking oil

For salad
85g (3oz) cucumber slices
1 small onion, sliced
1 large fresh tomato, sliced
110g (4oz) sliced radish, cut for salad
1 lettuce, washed
1 lemon, sliced

Method

1. Place the yoghurt, salt, turmeric powder, tomato purée, tandoori masala, garlic, chilli powder, ginger, green chillies and red colouring into a liquidizer and blend into a liquid.

2. Place the pork pieces in a large bowl, and pour the contents of the liquidizer over the pieces. Allow the meat to marinate in the mixture for the next 4 hours.

3. Place a wire rack in a baking tray. (The wire stand in the grill tray is very useful for this.)

4. Remove all the pork pieces from the mixture and place them on the wire rack.

5. Spread the 60ml (2fl oz) of oil evenly over all the pork pieces.

6. Cook at mark 5 (375°F or 190°C), on the middle shelf of a preheated oven, for about 45 minutes. Turn the pork pieces, remove all the excess liquid from the tray, and cook for a further 45 minutes. The excess liquid should be thrown away.

7. Take a large serving dish. Arrange the salad and lemon around the edge, and place the pork pieces in the middle of the salad.

8. Serve while the chops are still hot.

TANDOORI CHICKEN

Serves 4.

Preparation and cooking time: 6 hrs.

This is a mild chicken starter. It can be served cold or hot and is very useful for picnics. You will require a liquidizer or blender for this recipe.

900g (2lb) chicken pieces
90ml (3fl oz) plain yoghurt
5–6 drops of red food colouring
1 tsp salt
1 tsp turmeric powder
3 tsp tomato purée
2 tsp tandoori masala
55g (2oz) fresh garlic, peeled
55g (2oz) fresh ginger, peeled
5 green chillies
60ml (2fl oz) cooking oil

Method

1. Remove the skin from the chicken pieces. Place these pieces in a large pan.

2. Mix the yoghurt, food colouring, salt, turmeric powder, tomato purée, tandoori masala, garlic, ginger, and green chillies into a liquidizer and blend into a liquid. Pour this liquid over the chicken pieces.

3. Leave the mixture to marinate for 4 to 6 hours.

4. Place a wire rack in a baking tray. (The wire stand in the grill tray is very useful for this.) Remove the chicken pieces from the mixture and arrange them on the wire rack. Spread the cooking oil evenly on the chicken.

5. Cook at mark 5 (375°F or 190°C) in the middle shelf of a preheated oven, for about 30 minutes. Remove all the excess liquid and carry on cooking for another 20 minutes. Remove any further excess liquid, turn the chicken pieces and cook for a further 30 minutes. All the excess liquid should be thrown away.

6. Place chicken in serving dish.

TANDOORI FISH WITH SALAD

Serves 4.

Preparation and cooking time: 2 hrs. 45 mins.

This is an excellent mild starter for a special occasion. You will require a liquidizer or blender for this recipe.

120ml (4fl oz) plain yoghurt
1 tsp salt
1 tsp turmeric powder
2 tsp tomato purée
2 tsp tandoori masala
25g (1oz) fresh garlic, peeled
25g (1oz) fresh ginger, peeled
5–6 drops red food colouring
4 green chillies
675g (1¹/₂lb) cod fish, cut into 10cm (4 inch) long pieces
60ml (2fl oz) cooking oil

For salad
110g (4oz) cucumber slices
1 onion, sliced
2 fresh tomatoes, cut for salad
110g (4oz) sliced radish, cut for salad
Some fresh lettuce, washed
1 lemon, sliced

Method

1. Place the yoghurt, salt, turmeric powder, tomato purée, tandoori masala, garlic, ginger, food colouring and green chillies into a liquidizer and blend into a liquid.

2. Place the fish pieces in a large pan. Pour the blended liquid over the fish and let the mixture marinate for about 2 hours.

3. Place a wire rack in a baking tray. (The wire stand in the grill tray is very useful for this.)

4. Remove all the fish pieces from the pan and place them on the wire rack.

5. Spread the oil evenly on the fish pieces.

6. Cook at mark 5 (375°F or 190°C) on the middle shelf of a preheated oven for about 35 minutes.

7. Arrange the salad and lemon around the sides of a large serving dish and place the fish in the centre.

8. Serve while the fish is hot.

BEEF KEBABS

Serves 4.

Preparation and cooking time: 1 hr.

The word *kebab* has a different meaning in Indian cookery. Indian kebabs are like burgers and are made of mince mixed with spices. Beef kebabs are usually served as starters. They also make excellent snacks for high teas, parties and barbecues.

450g (1lb) minced beef
1 large onion, finely chopped
1 tsp garam masala
1 tsp tomato purée
1 tsp salt
1 tsp tandoori masala
$^1/_2$ tsp chilli powder
1 tsp whole jeera (cumin seeds)
5–6 drops red food colouring

Method
1. Mix all the above ingredients thoroughly in a large mixing bowl.
2. Divide the mixture into about 8 equal parts.
3. Roll each part into a ball and then roll it flat, about 0.5cm ($^1/_4$ inch) thick, 7cm (2 to 3 inches) in diameter, like a burger.
4. Grill each side for about 10 minutes under a hot grill.
5. Serve while hot.

LAMB KEBABS WITH SALAD

Serves 4.

Preparation and cooking time: 1hr 35 mins.

Lamb kebabs are made of minced lamb mixed with spices, and are usually served as a starter. They can also be served at parties or with a glass of wine, as a snack to accompany the drink. For this recipe you need a liquidizer.

25g (1oz) fresh garlic, peeled
25g (1oz) fresh ginger, peeled
4 green chillies
450g (1lb) minced lamb
1 large onion, finely chopped
1 tsp salt
2 tsp tandoori masala
$^1/_2$ tsp chilli powder
1 tsp whole jeera (cumin seeds)
3 tsp tomato purée

For salad
Fresh crispy lettuce
85g (3oz) cucumber, sliced
1 small onion, sliced
2 fresh tomatoes, sliced for salad
1 lemon, sliced

Method

1. Process the garlic, fresh ginger and green chillies in a liquidizer until finely chopped.
2. Mix the contents of the liquidizer, mince, onion, salt, tandoori masala, chilli powder, jeera and tomato purée in a large mixing bowl. Mix everything together well.
3. Divide the mixture into roughly 8 equal portions. Shape each of these portions into sausage type shapes. These shapes are called kebabs.
4. Place these kebabs on the wire stand of a grill pan and cook under a hot grill for about 25 minutes turning sides of the kebabs every 5 to 7 minutes. Take extreme care when changing sides so as not to break the kebabs.
5. Arrange the salad on one side of a serving dish, and arrange the cooked kebabs on the other side of the dish.
6. Serve while hot.

SPARE RIBS COOKED IN MICROWAVE OVEN

Serves 4.

Preparation and cooking time: 40 mins.

If you are fond of pork and want to try something new on the family or friends, then this dish is extremely useful. These spare ribs can be served with salad or rice. For this recipe you can either buy small spare ribs or get your butcher to cut large ribs into halves. This recipe needs a microwave oven and a deep frying pan or wok.

600ml (20fl oz) cooking oil for frying
900g (2lb) small spare ribs
2 tsp tomato purée
2 tsp tomato ketchup
1 tsp garlic powder
4 tsp soy sauce
90ml (3fl oz) water

Method
1. Heat the oil to a high temperature in a wok or deep frying pan and then deep fry the ribs until they are golden brown. This will usually take about 15 to 20 minutes.
2. Transfer the fried meat into a 25cm (10 inch) pyrex or microwave dish.
3. Mix the tomato purée, tomato ketchup, garlic powder, soy sauce and water together and pour the mixture on top of the ribs. Place the dish in a microwave oven and cook for 10 minutes at full power.
4. Serve while hot.

TOMATO SOUP

Serves 4.

Preparation and cooking time: 20 mins.

Indian tomato soup is a heavily spiced version of English tomato soup. It is one of the few vegetarian starters in Indian cookery and is a very light and thin soup. Like all soups, it can be served with bread or a roll.

450g (1lb) ripe tomatoes
30ml (1fl oz) cooking oil
6 whole cloves
$^1/_2$ tsp whole rai (black mustard seeds)
$^1/_4$ tsp hing (asafoetida)
1 tsp salt
1 tsp turmeric powder
1 tsp chilli powder
2 tsp sugar
450ml (15fl oz) water

Method
1. Wash all the tomatoes and cut them into very small pieces.
2. Heat the oil in a pan and add cloves, whole rai and asafoetida. Fry for a few seconds.
3. Add the tomatoes, salt, turmeric powder, chilli powder and the sugar. Reduce the heat, cover the pan and simmer gently for about 7 minutes.
4. Now add the water, mix well and bring to the boil. Allow it to simmer for a further 10 minutes.
5. Transfer the soup to a soup bowl; remove the cloves with a spoon and serve while hot.

POTATO KACHORIS
(Potato balls in chapatti flour)

Makes about 8 kachoris.

Preparation and cooking time: 1 hr.

This dish is very similar to samosas, but the pastry is made of chapatti flour, rather than plain flour. It can be served as a starter or at high teas and parties. Any left-over filling can be used for toasted sandwiches. For this recipe you need a deep frying pan or wok.

For filling
30ml (1fl oz) cooking oil
$^1/_2$ tsp whole rai (black mustard seeds)
1 large onion, finely chopped
450g (1lb) peeled potatoes, finely diced
1 tsp salt
1 tsp turmeric powder
1 tsp chilli powder
60ml (2fl oz) water
15ml ($^1/_2$fl oz) lemon juice

For pastry
225g (8oz) white chapatti flour, sieved
120ml (4fl oz) water
55g (2oz) chapatti flour for rolling out
600ml (20fl oz) cooking oil for frying

Method

1. In a pan, heat the oil to a high temperature. Add rai and let it cook for a few seconds. Add the onion and cook until the onion is golden brown. Add the potatoes, salt, turmeric powder and chilli powder. Stir and cook for about 2 minutes.

2. Add the 60ml (2fl oz) of water, lower the heat, cover the pan and allow it to simmer for about 10 minutes. Then add the lemon juice, mix well, and switch off the heat. Let it cool.

3. Place the chapatti flour in a big bowl; add half of the 120ml (4fl oz) of water and mix well. Continue adding small amounts of water at a time and mixing well until a soft, medium dough is formed. Divide this dough into roughly 8 equal pieces. Shape these pieces into round balls.

4. Sprinkle some dry flour onto each ball, and roll it into a circle 13cm (about 5 inches) in diameter. Place 4 teaspoonfuls of the potato filling in the middle of one half of the rolled chapatti. Lift the other half to cover the filling completely and squeeze the edges together, thus making a semi-circle shape with the filling in the middle. Lift it carefully and place it on one side. Repeat this with all the 8 balls. These filled balls are called kachoris.

5. Heat the 600ml (20fl oz) of oil to a high temperature, in a deep frying pan or wok. Now add 2 kachoris at a time and fry each side of the kachori until it is golden brown. This will usually take about 3 to 4 minutes for each side. Fry all the kachoris in this way.

6. Serve the kachoris while they are hot.

MOONG KACHORIS
(Moong dhal balls in chapatti flour)

Makes about 8 kachoris.

Preparation and cooking time: 10 hrs.

This dish is very similar to samosas, but the pastry is made of chapatti flour, rather than plain flour. Moong dhal kachoris are more popular with vegetarians. It can be served as a starter or at high teas and parties. Any leftover filling can be used for toasted sandwiches. For this recipe you need a deep frying pan or wok.

For filling
225g (8oz) skinless, split moong dhal
1200ml (40fl oz) water for soaking
30ml (1fl oz) cooking oil
$^1/_2$ tsp whole rai (black mustard seeds)
$^1/_2$ tsp whole jeera (cumin seeds)
$1^1/_2$ tsp salt
1 tsp turmeric powder
1 tsp chilli powder
1 tsp garam masala
300ml (10fl oz) water
30ml (1fl oz) lemon juice

For pastry
225g (8oz) white chapatti flour, sieved
120ml (4fl oz) water
55g (2oz) chapatti flour for rolling out
600ml (20fl oz) cooking oil for frying

Method

1. Wash the moong dhal making sure that little stones are not left in the dhal. (See page 16.)

2. Soak the dhal overnight in the 1200ml (40fl oz) of water.

3. Drain the water from the dhal in the morning.

4. In a pan, heat the oil to a high temperature. Add rai and jeera and cook for a few seconds. Add the dhal, salt, turmeric powder, chilli powder and garam masala. Stir and cook for about 2 minutes.

5. Add the 300ml (10fl oz) of water, lower the heat, cover the pan and allow it to simmer for about 20 minutes. Now add the lemon juice, mix well and switch off the heat. Let this filling cool down.

6. Place the chapatti flour in a big bowl; add half of the 120ml (4fl oz) of water and mix well. Continue adding small amounts of water at a time and mixing well until a soft, medium dough is formed. Divide this dough into roughly 8 equal parts. Shape these parts into round balls.

7. Sprinkle some dry flour into the balls, and roll each ball into a 13cm (5 inch) diameter round shape. Place 4 teaspoonfuls of the moong dhal filling in the middle of one half of the rolled chapatti. Lift the other half to cover the filling completely and squeeze the edges together, thus making a semi-circle shape with the filling in the middle. Lift it carefully and place it on one side. Repeat this with all the 8 balls. These filled balls are called kachoris.

8. Heat the 600ml (20fl oz) of oil to a high temperature in a deep frying pan or wok. Now add 2 kachoris at a time and fry each side of the kachori until it is golden brown. This will usually take about 3 to 4 minutes for each side. Fry all the kachoris in this way.

9. Serve the kachoris while they are hot.

PORK TIKKA

(Pork pieces, marinated and cooked in yoghurt)

Serves 4.

Preparation and cooking time: 8 hrs 50 mins.

All tikka dishes make very good starters and snacks. As starters they are usually served with a salad. For this recipe you need a liquidizer.

25g (1oz) fresh garlic, peeled
25g (1oz) fresh ginger, peeled
4 green chillies
180ml (6fl oz) natural, fresh yoghurt
2 tsp soy sauce
1 tsp salt
2 tsp tomato purée
1 tsp turmeric powder
1 tsp chilli powder
1 tsp red food colouring
15ml (¹/₂fl oz) lemon juice
340g (12oz) pork steak
60ml (2fl oz) cooking oil
120ml (4fl oz) water

Method

1. Mix the garlic, ginger, chillies, yoghurt, soy sauce, salt, tomato purée, turmeric powder, chilli powder, red food colouring and lemon juice in a liquidizer and blend it into a liquid.
2. Cut the pork steak into small 1cm ($^{1}/_{2}$ inch) cubes.
3. Place the pork pieces in a large pan and then pour the blended mixture on the pork pieces.
4. Leave the mixture to marinate for about 8 hours.
5. Heat the oil in a large pan to a high temperature and then add the pork with all its spiced liquid. Stir continuously and cook for about 10 minutes.
6. Add the 120ml (4fl oz) of water, cover the pan, lower the heat and let it simmer for about 35 minutes, stirring every 5 to 7 minutes.
7. Remove the cover of the pan, raise the heat and let the water evaporate, leaving a rather dry pork tikka. This will usually take about 3 to 4 minutes.
8. Serve hot, with salad or on its own.

CHICKEN TIKKA
(Chicken pieces, marinated and cooked in yoghurt)

Serves 4.

Preparation and cooking time: 8 hrs 40 mins.

All tikka dishes make very good starters and snacks. As starters they
are usually served with a salad. For this recipe you need a liquidizer
and a sharp knife.

25g (1oz) fresh garlic, peeled
25g (1oz) fresh ginger, peeled
4 green chillies
180ml (6fl oz) natural, fresh yoghurt
2 tsp soy sauce
1 tsp salt
2 tsp tomato purée
1 tsp turmeric powder
1 tsp chilli powder
1 tsp red food colouring
15 ml (¹/₂fl oz) lemon juice
670g (1¹/₂lb) chicken pieces
60ml (2fl oz) cooking oil
60ml (2fl oz) water

Method

1. Place the garlic, ginger, chillies, yoghurt, soy sauce, salt, tomato purée, turmeric powder, chilli powder, red colouring and lemon juice in a liquidizer and blend into a liquid.
2. Remove the skin from the chicken pieces and chop into 2.5cm (about 1 inch) long pieces.
3. Place the chicken pieces in a large pan and pour over the blended mixture.
4. Leave this mixture to marinate for about 8 hours.
5. Heat the oil in a large pan to a high temperature and then add the chicken with all its spiced liquid. Stir continuously and cook for about 10 minutes.
6. Add the 60ml (2fl oz) of water, cover the pan, lower the heat and let it simmer for about 25 minutes, stirring every 5 to 7 minutes.
7. Remove the cover of the pan, raise the heat and let the water evaporate, leaving a rather dry chicken dish. This will usually take about 3 to 4 minutes.
8. Serve hot, with salad or on its own.

BEEF TIKKA

(Beef pieces, marinated and cooked in yoghurt)

Serves 4.

Preparation and cooking time: 9 hrs.

All tikka dishes make very good starters and snacks. As starters they are usually served with a salad. For this recipe you need a liquidizer.

25g (1oz) fresh garlic, peeled
25g (1oz) fresh ginger, peeled
4 green chillies
180ml (6fl oz) natural, fresh yoghurt
2 tsp soy sauce
1 tsp salt
2 tsp tomato purée
1 tsp turmeric powder
1 tsp chilli powder
1 tsp red food colouring
15ml ($^{1}/_{2}$fl oz) lemon juice
340g (12oz) beef steak
60ml (2fl oz) cooking oil
180ml (6fl oz) water

Method

1. Place the garlic, ginger, chillies, yoghurt, soy sauce, salt, tomato purée, turmeric powder, chilli powder, red colouring and lemon juice in a liquidizer and blend into a liquid.
2. Cut the beef steak into small, 1cm ($^1/_2$ inch) cubes.
3. Place the beef pieces in a large pan, and then pour the blended mixture onto the beef pieces.
4. Leave this mixture to marinate for about 8 hours.
5. Heat the oil in a large pan to a high temperature, and then add the beef with all its spiced liquid. Stir continuously, and cook for about 10 minutes.
6. Add the 180ml (6fl oz) of water, cover the pan, lower the heat and let it simmer for about 45 minutes, stirring every 5 to 7 minutes.
7. Remove the cover of the pan, raise the heat and let the water evaporate, leaving a rather dry beef dish. This will usually take about 3 to 4 minutes.
8. Serve hot, with salad or on its own.

LAMB TIKKA
(Lamb pieces, marinated and cooked in yoghurt)

Serves 4.

Preparation and cooking time: 9 hrs.

All tikka dishes make very good starters and snacks. As starters they are usually served with a salad. For this recipe you need a liquidizer.

25g (1oz) fresh garlic, peeled
25g (1oz) fresh ginger, peeled
4 green chillies
180ml (6fl oz) natural, fresh yoghurt
2 tsp soy sauce
1 tsp salt
2 tsp tomato purée
1 tsp turmeric powder
1 tsp chilli powder
1 tsp red food colouring
15ml ($^{1}/_{2}$fl oz) lemon juice
340g (12oz) diced lamb
60ml (2fl oz) cooking oil
150ml (5fl oz) water

Method

1. Place the garlic, ginger, chillies, yoghurt, soy sauce, salt, tomato purée, turmeric powder, chilli powder, red colouring and lemon juice in a liquidizer and blend into a liquid.
2. Place the lamb pieces in a large pan, and pour the blended mixture onto the lamb pieces.
3. Leave this mixture to marinate for about 8 hours.
4. Heat the oil in a large pan to a high temperature and then add the lamb with all its spiced liquid. Stir continuously, and cook for about 10 minutes.
5. Add the 150ml (5fl oz) of water, cover the pan, lower the heat and let it simmer for about 40 minutes, stirring every 5 to 7 minutes.
6. Remove the cover of the pan, raise the heat and let the water evaporate, leaving a rather dry lamb dish. This will usually take about 3 to 4 minutes.
7. Serve hot, with salad or on its own.

2

SAVOURY SNACKS

MATHI
(A savoury biscuit made with plain flour)

Makes about 60 mathis.

Preparation and cooking time: 2 hrs.

This is a savoury biscuit, which is usually served with a cup of tea or coffee. It can also be used in packed lunches, picnics, or at parties. In fact it makes a good substitute for biscuits, especially if you like savoury snacks. Cooked mathis, like biscuits, can be stored in an airtight tin for up to 6 or 7 weeks. For this recipe you need a wok or deep frying pan.

450g (1lb) plain flour
85g (3oz) butter or soft margarine
$^1/_2$ tsp salt
1 tsp ground black pepper
90ml (3fl oz) water
1200ml (40fl oz) cooking oil for frying

Method

1. Sieve the plain flour into a large mixing bowl, and add the butter (or margarine), salt and ground pepper and mix well.
2. Mix in the water gradually until a medium soft dough is formed. (Make sure that you do not add too much water at a time.)
3. Divide the mixture into little balls, about 4cm (1^1/$_2$ inches) in diameter.
4. Roll each ball into a circle about 7cm (3 inches) in diameter and about 2mm (^{1}/$_8$ inch) thick.
5. Make a couple of 2.5cm (1 inch) marks on the rolled mathi, with a sharp knife. The knife should only penetrate the top and not cut through the whole thickness of the mathi.
6. Lay the rolled balls out separately.
7. Heat the oil in a wok or a deep frying pan to a high temperature. When it is hot, add about 3 mathis at a time and let them deep fry for a few seconds. Soon they will float to the top; now turn them and fry the mathis until they are golden brown all over. (The browning process on each mathi should take about 2 minutes; if it takes less time the oil is too hot and therefore the heat should be lowered.)
8. Let the mathis cool and then store them in an airtight tin.

VIDA
(A savoury snack made with cornflour)

Serves 4.

Preparation and cooking time: 12 hrs 40 mins.

This is an unusual snack, although common in the Gujarat state of India. For this recipe you need a deep frying pan, or wok, and a liquidizer.

225g (8oz) cornflour
90ml (3fl oz) yoghurt
120ml (4fl oz) water
55g (2oz) fresh garlic, peeled
55g (2oz) fresh ginger, peeled
4 green chillies
$^{1}/_{2}$ tsp salt
$^{1}/_{2}$ tsp turmeric powder
$^{1}/_{2}$ tsp chilli powder
600ml (20fl oz) cooking oil for frying

Method

1. Sieve the cornflour into a bowl. Add the yoghurt and mix well. Add water gradually and continue to mix until a stiff dough is formed. Cover the bowl and leave for about 12 hours.

2. Process the garlic, ginger and chillies in a liquidizer until finely chopped.

3. Add the salt, turmeric powder, chilli powder and liquidizer contents into the stiff dough. Mix everything together. Take a small amount of dough at a time; shape it first into a ball and then pat the ball into a circle about 4cm ($1^1/_2$ inches) in diameter and 0.5cm ($^1/_4$ inch) thick. Wet the palms of your hands with water occasionally while doing this. These shapes are called vidas.

4. Heat the oil in a wok or deep frying pan to a high temperature, and fry the vidas (5 to 7 at a time) in the oil. Deep fry the vidas on a low heat. The frying process should take about 3–4 minutes; if it takes less then the oil is too hot. When the vidas are golden brown place them in a serving dish and serve while hot.

CHAVADA

(Mixture of many spiced nuts and seeds)

Makes about 1.35kg (3lb) of chavada.

Preparation and cooking time: 12 hrs.

Chavada is a mixture of deep fried nuts and dhal, and is used as a savoury snack, usually served with a cup of tea or coffee. It can also be used in packed lunches, picnics or parties. Chavada can be stored in an airtight tin for about 4 to 5 weeks and used as and when needed. For this recipe you need a deep frying pan or wok.

450g (1lb) chana dhal
1200ml (40fl oz) cooking oil for frying
225g (¹/₂lb) puffed rice
225g (¹/₂lb) ready salted crisps
225g (¹/₂lb) ready salted peanuts
1 tsp salt
1 tsp turmeric powder
1 tsp chilli powder

Method

1. Soak the chana dhal in about 2 litres (70fl oz) of water overnight.
2. Drain off all the water from the dhal and spread on kitchen roll paper.
3. Heat the oil in a large wok, or frying pan to a high temperature. Place small amounts of dhal in the oil, and deep fry until the dhal seeds are golden brown, or eat one of the dhal seeds: it should taste hard and crunchy. Remove the dhal with a sieve and spread the fried dhal on some fresh kitchen roll paper. Fry all the dhal in this way.
4. Now fry the rice in the hot oil, again only a small quantity at a time. Puffed rice grains fry very quickly, so keep the pot and sieve ready.
5. Mix the fried rice, dhal, crisps, peanuts, salt, turmeric powder and chilli powder in a large pot. Mix well, and transfer the contents to an airtight tin. This will keep the chavada fresh for about a month.
6. Serve as and when needed, making sure that the lid of the tin is kept well closed, after use.

HANDVA
(Spicy 'cake' type snack made from rice flour)

Serves 4.

Preparation and cooking time: 50 hrs.

This is a savoury snack usually served at high teas, parties or picnics.
It can be stored in the fridge for a couple of days and heated as and
when required. For this recipe you need a liquidizer, a whisk and a
20cm (8 inch) cake tin.

90ml (3fl oz) natural yoghurt
90ml (3fl oz) water
340g (12oz) dhokra flour (mixture of ground rice and ground
    chana dhal, available from most Indian grocery shops)
25g (1oz) fresh garlic, peeled
3 green chillies
1 tsp salt
1 tsp turmeric powder
$^1/_2$ tsp chilli powder
$^1/_4$ tsp baking powder
60ml (2fl oz) cooking oil
$^1/_4$ tsp whole jeera (cumin seeds)
$^1/_4$ tsp whole rai (black mustard seeds)
$^1/_4$ tsp hing (asafoetida)

Method

1. Mix the yoghurt and water together with a whisk. This mixture is called lassi.
2. Mix the dhokra flour and lassi together well, and leave to ferment in a warm spot, for 48 hours. The airing cupboard is ideal for this purpose.
3. Place the garlic and chillies into a liquidizer, and chop very finely.
4. After fermentation, add the salt, turmeric powder, chilli powder, baking powder and liquidizer contents to the dhokra mixture. Mix well.
5. Heat the oil in a frying pan to a high temperature, and add the jeera, rai and hing (asafoetida). Cook for a few seconds.
6. Transfer half of the heated oil mixture to a 20cm (8 inch) cake tin. Add the dhokra flour mixture and then pour the remaining oil mixture on top of the dhokra mixture.
7. Bake in a preheated oven at gas mark 2 (300°F or 150°C) for about $2^1/_2$ hours on the middle shelf of the oven.
8. Leave the handva to cool for a few minutes and then cut into small pieces for serving. The cut pieces can be stored in a fridge, and warmed when needed for about 20 minutes, in a preheated oven before serving.

CHANA DHAL FRIED
(Deep fried gram seeds)

Makes about 900g (2lb) of dhal.

Preparation and cooking time: 12 hrs.

This is a deep fried gram dhal, usually served with a cup of tea or coffee. It can also be munched while watching television or just relaxing. Like chavada, fried chana dhal can be stored in an airtight tin for 4 to 5 weeks and used as and when needed. For this recipe you need a deep wok or frying pan.

900g (2lb) chana dhal
1200ml (40fl oz) cooking oil for frying
1 tsp salt
1 tsp turmeric powder
1 tsp chilli powder

Method
1. Soak the chana dhal in about 2 litres (70fl oz) of water overnight.
2. Drain all the water from the dhal, and spread the dhal on some clean kitchen roll paper.
3. Heat the oil in a wok or deep frying pan to a high temperature. Add small amounts of the dhal to the oil and deep fry until the dhal seeds are golden brown. Another method of checking if they are ready is to eat one of the dhal seeds. It should feel hard and crunchy. Remove the fried dhal with a sieve and spread it on some fresh clean kitchen roll paper. Repeat with the remaining dhal.
4. Add the salt, turmeric powder, and chilli powder to the dhal and mix well. Transfer the contents to an airtight tin. This will keep the dhal fresh for about a month.

SAVOURY PEANUTS

Makes about 900g (2lb) peanuts.

Preparation and cooking time: 20 mins.

Indians like spices in most of their snacks, and peanuts are no exception. They are usually served at parties, or with a glass of wine or a cup of tea. Savoury peanuts can be stored in an airtight tin for up to 3 weeks, and used as and when needed. For this recipe you need a wok or deep frying pan.

600ml (20fl oz) cooking oil
900g (2lb) peanuts
1 tsp salt
1 tsp chilli powder
1 tsp black pepper powder

Method
1. Heat the oil to a high temperature, in a wok or deep frying pan. Once the oil is hot, reduce the heat and add a handful of peanuts. Deep fry until they are golden brown. This will usually take about 10 to 15 seconds. Remove the peanuts with a sieve and spread them on kitchen roll paper.
2. Repeat this with all the peanuts.
3. In a large mixing bowl, mix well the peanuts, salt, chilli powder and pepper powder.
4. Let the peanuts cool, and then transfer the contents to an airtight tin. They can be stored this way for up to 3 weeks.

SAVOURY CASHEW NUTS

Makes about 900g (2lb) cashew nuts.

Preparation and cooking time: 20 mins.

Savoury cashew nuts taste excellent and are well worth a try. Like peanuts, they are usually served at parties, or with a glass of wine or a cup of tea. They can be stored in an airtight tin for up to 2 weeks, and used as and when needed. For this recipe you need a wok or deep frying pan.

600ml (20fl oz) cooking oil
900g (2lb) cashew nuts
1 tsp salt
1 tsp chilli powder
1 tsp black pepper powder

Method
1. Heat the oil to a high temperature, in a wok or a deep frying pan. Once the oil is hot, reduce the heat and add a handful of cashew nuts. Deep fry until they are golden brown. This will usually take about 10 to 15 seconds. Remove the cashew nuts with a sieve and spread them on kitchen roll paper.
2. Repeat this with all the cashew nuts.
3. In a large mixing bowl, mix the cashew nuts, salt, chilli powder and pepper powder well together.
4. Let the cashew nuts cool, and then transfer the contents to an airtight tin. They can be stored this way for up to 2 weeks.

POPPADUMS

Poppadums come in three main varieties – made from rice flour, moong dhal flour or urad dhal flour. Within these three varieties there are a number of sub-varieties, each having different quantities of spices mixed in them. When you buy poppadums, do check on whether they are hot or mild. It may be an idea to try different types to find out which you prefer. It is very difficult to recommend one particular variety, as it very much depends on individual taste.

Poppadums can be deep fried (one at a time, in about 1 litre/40fl oz) of cooking oil heated to a high temperature), or grilled like toast. It takes about half a minute to grill each side, but the deep fry method is much quicker, taking literally seconds, once the oil is heated.

It is normally recommended that rice poppadums should be deep fried, but dhal poppadums taste good done either way. In most restaurants, only fried poppadums are served.

3

MEAT, FISH AND EGG CURRIES

RED CHORI AND MINCE CURRY

(Mince with red lentil-type seeds)

Serves 4.

Preparation and cooking time: 10 hrs 30 mins.

If you do not like beans but would like to try something similar to chilli con carne, then this is the dish for you. This mince curry is usually served with rice or chapattis. It can also be served with chips. For this recipe you need a liquidizer.

NB The chori must be boiled for about 45 minutes as indicated in the recipe otherwise it could cause indigestion.

55g (2oz) red chori
450ml (15fl oz) water for boiling red chori
10g ($^1/_2$oz) fresh garlic, peeled
25g (1oz) fresh ginger, peeled
2 green chillies
30ml (1fl oz) cooking oil
1 large onion, finely chopped
1 tsp tomato purée
$^1/_2$ tsp turmeric powder
$^1/_2$ tsp chilli powder
$^1/_2$ tsp tandoori masala
1 tsp garam masala
$^1/_2$ tsp salt
4 tsp soy sauce
225g (8oz) minced beef
300ml (10fl oz) water for cooking
Small amount green dhanyia (coriander), chopped

Method

1. Wash the red chori, like all dhals, and leave to soak in about 600ml (20fl oz) of cold water for about 8 hours. (See page 16 on how to wash dhals.)

2. Strain the chori and put in a pan. Add the 450ml (15fl oz) of water. Place the pan on a hot ring, and bring the water to the boil. When the water has started to boil, cover the pan, lower the heat and simmer for a further 45 minutes.

3. Place the garlic, ginger and green chillies into a liquidizer and chop very finely.

4. Heat the cooking oil in a large pan to a high temperature. Add the onion and cook until it is golden brown.

5. Add the contents of the liquidizer, tomato purée, turmeric powder, chilli powder, tandoori masala, garam masala, salt and soy sauce. Cook this mixture for about 2 minutes.

6. Now add the boiled chori and the mince. Simmer gently for another 15 minutes stirring every 5 minutes.

7. Add the 300ml (10fl oz) of water, cover the pan and let it simmer for a further 45 minutes. Stir every 5 minutes.

8. Transfer the curry into a serving dish and garnish with fresh coriander. Serve while hot.

MINCED LAMB CURRY

Serves 4.

Preparation and cooking time: 50 mins.

This is a dry curry usually served with chapattis or pitta bread. It also makes excellent filling for toasted sandwiches. Bay leaves may be added to give the curry a nice fragrance and a slightly sharper taste. For this recipe you need a liquidizer.

10g (¹/₂oz) fresh garlic, peeled
25g (1oz) fresh ginger, peeled
3 green chillies
60ml (2fl oz) cooking oil
1 large onion, finely chopped
2 tsp tomato purée
1 tsp turmeric powder
1 tsp chilli powder
2 tsp tandoori masala
1 tsp garam masala
1 tsp salt
2 bay leaves (optional)
340g (12oz) minced lamb
600ml (20fl oz) water
Small amount green dhanyia (coriander), chopped

Method

1. Place the garlic, ginger, and green chillies into a liquidizer and chop finely.
2. Heat the oil in a pan and add the chopped onion. Cook the onion until it is golden brown. Now add the liquidizer contents, tomato purée, turmeric powder, chilli powder, tandoori masala, garam masala, salt (and bay leaves if used). Cook for a further 5 minutes, stirring continuously.
3. Add the mince, and cook for a further 5 minutes, stirring continuously.
4. Add the water, cover the pan, reduce the heat and simmer gently for a further 30 minutes, stirring every 5 to 7 minutes.
5. Transfer the contents to a serving dish and garnish with fresh green coriander. Serve while hot.
6. The bay leaves (if used) are discarded while eating and left on the plate.

LAMB'S LIVER CURRY

Serves 4.

Preparation and cooking time: 1 hr 10 mins.

This liver curry is usually eaten on its own, or served with chapattis or bread but is not served with rice. It is normally very mild but fresh green chillies can be added to make it slightly hot. For this recipe you need a liquidizer.

10g (¹/₂oz) fresh garlic, peeled
25g (1oz) fresh ginger, peeled
3 green chillies (optional for hot curry)
55g (2oz) tinned tomatoes
30ml (1fl oz) cooking oil
1 large onion, finely chopped
450g (1lb) lamb's liver, cut into small pieces
¹/₂ tsp turmeric powder
1 tsp tomato purée
¹/₂ tsp chilli powder
1 tsp tandoori masala
1 tsp salt
¹/₂ tsp garam masala
300ml (10fl oz) water
Small amount green dhanyia (coriander), chopped

Method

1. Preheat the oven to mark 5 (375°F or 190°C). Place the garlic, ginger, green chillies (if used), and tomatoes in a liquidizer and blend them into a thick paste.

2. Place the oil in a pan. When hot, add the chopped onion. Cook the onion until it is golden brown. Add the contents of the liquidizer, liver pieces, turmeric powder, tomato purée, chilli powder, tandoori masala, salt and garam masala. Cook for about 10 minutes, stirring constantly. Place the curry in a casserole. Add water and stir.

3. Cover the casserole, and cook on the middle shelf of the preheated oven for about 45 to 50 minutes.

4. Garnish with green dhanyia (coriander) and serve while hot.

DRY BHOONA LAMB CHOPS

Serves 4.

Preparation and cooking time: 1 hr.

This is a very dry and mild curry which can be served with fried rice, or even mashed potatoes or chips. For this recipe you need a wok or deep frying pan.

8 lamb chops
90ml (3fl oz) cooking oil
$^1/_2$ tsp whole jeera (cumin seeds)
$^1/_2$ tsp whole rai (black mustard seeds)
225g (8oz) onions, finely chopped
2 green chillies, finely chopped
110g (4oz) tinned tomatoes, finely chopped
$1^1/_2$ tsp salt
1 tsp turmeric powder
$1^1/_2$ tsp garam masala
$^1/_2$ tsp chilli powder
120ml (4fl oz) water
Small amount green dhania (coriander), chopped

Method

1. Cut the fat from the lamb chops.
2. In a wok, or deep frying pan, heat the oil to a high temperature. Add the jeera and rai and let it cook for a few seconds. Add the chopped onions and the green chillies. Stir continuously and cook until the onions are golden brown. Add the tomatoes and cook for about a minute. Add the salt, turmeric powder, garam masala and chilli powder. Cook this spicy mixture for about another minute.
3. Add the lamb chops. Mix well, cover the pan, lower the heat and let it simmer for about 10 minutes, stirring every 3 to 4 minutes.
4. Add the water, mix well and simmer for another 40 minutes stirring every 8 to 10 minutes.
5. Transfer the contents to a serving dish and garnish with the green dhanyia (coriander).

LAMB VINDALOO
(Hot lamb and potato curry)

Serves 4.

Preparation and cooking time: 1 hr.

This is a very hot curry usually served with rice, chapattis or parothas.

450g (1lb) potatoes
60ml (2fl oz) cooking oil
1 large onion, finely chopped
6 green chillies, finely chopped
3 tsp tomato purée
2 tsp turmeric powder
2 tsp chilli powder
1 tsp garlic powder
1 tsp ginger powder
2 tsp salt
2 tsp garam masala
450g (1lb) diced lamb
450ml (15fl oz) water
Small amount green dhanyia (coriander), chopped

Method

1. Peel the potatoes and cut into largish pieces (about 2.5cm/1 inch cubes).
2. Heat the oil to a high temperature in a large pan. Add the onion and chillies, and cook, stirring continuously, until the onion is golden brown.
3. Add the tomato purée, turmeric powder, chilli powder, garlic powder, ginger powder, salt, garam masala and the diced lamb. Mix well, lower the heat and simmer gently for about 5 minutes, stirring every 2 to 3 minutes.
4. Add the water and let the lamb simmer for about 35 minutes, stirring every 5 to 7 minutes.
5. Add the potatoes and simmer for another 20 minutes, stirring every 5 to 7 minutes.
6. Transfer the contents to a serving dish and garnish with green dhanyia (coriander).

CHICKEN VINDALOO
(Hot chicken and potato curry)

Serves 4.

Preparation and cooking time: 50 mins.

This is a very hot curry usually served with rice, chapattis or parothas. For this recipe you need a liquidizer and a chopper.

450g (1lb) potatoes
900g (2lb) fresh chicken
1 large onion
6 green chillies
10g ($^1/_2$oz) fresh ginger
10g ($^1/_2$oz) fresh garlic
60ml (2fl oz) cooking oil
3 tsp tomato purée
2 tsp turmeric powder
2 tsp chilli powder
1 tsp garlic powder
1 tsp ginger powder
2 tsp salt
2 tsp garam masala
2 tsp tandoori powder
150ml (5fl oz) water
Small amount green dhanyia (coriander), chopped

Method

1. Peel the potatoes and cut into largish pieces (about 2.5cm/1 inch cubes).

2. Remove the skin from the chicken pieces and chop the chicken into small (about 8cm/3 inch long) pieces.

3. Place the onion, chillies, ginger and garlic in a liquidizer and process until finely chopped.

4. Heat the oil to a high temperature in a large pan. Add the processed onions, chillies, ginger and garlic and cook, stirring continuously, until the onion is golden brown.

5. Add the tomato purée, turmeric powder, chilli powder, garlic powder, ginger powder, salt, garam masala, tandoori powder and the chicken. Mix well, lower the heat and simmer gently for about 10 minutes, stirring every 2 to 3 minutes.

6. Add the water and let the chicken simmer for about 20 minutes, stirring every 5 to 7 minutes.

7. Add the potatoes and simmer for another 20 minutes, stirring every 5 to 7 minutes.

8. Transfer the contents to a serving dish and garnish with green dhanyia (coriander).

9. The bones are discarded while eating and left on the plate.

BEEF KOFTAS
(Beef meatballs)

Serves 4.

Preparation and cooking time: 1 hr 50 mins.

Beef koftas are particularly good if you like mince dishes. They can be served with rice or chapattis. They can also be served with 'English side dishes' such as boiled potatoes, cabbage or cauliflower. For this recipe you need a liquidizer.

25g (1oz) fresh garlic, peeled
25g (1oz) fresh ginger, peeled
3 green chillies
450g (1lb) minced beef
1 tsp salt
$^1/_2$ tsp chilli powder
2 tsp tandoori masala
1 tsp garam masala
2 tsp tomato purée
Small amount green dhanyia (coriander), chopped
30ml (1fl oz) cooking oil
2 medium sized onions, finely chopped
55g (2oz) plum peeled tomatoes
300ml (10fl oz) water

Method

1. Place the garlic, ginger and green chillies into a liquidizer and process until finely chopped.

2. Mix the contents of the liquidizer with the mince, salt, chilli powder, tandoori masala, garam masala, tomato purée and fresh dhanyia and mix well. Shape the mixture into small meatballs approximately 5cm (2 inches) in diameter, and place them on a tray. Cover the tray.

3. Heat the oil in a large cooking pan. Add the onions and fry until they are golden brown. Now add the tomatoes and cook for a further 2 minutes.

4. Gently place 6 to 8 meatballs in the pan. Cover the pan, lower the heat and simmer for about 20 minutes. The meatballs will shrink in size and become golden brown. Carefully remove these balls from the onion and tomato mixture and place them on one side. Add another 6 to 8 fresh mince balls to the onion and tomato mixture, cover and simmer again for about the same period. Repeat this process until all the meatballs are done.

5. Now add all the meatballs to the onion and tomato mixture. Stir very gently and simmer for a further 50 minutes. Add the water, bring it to the boil, and simmer for a further 45 minutes, stirring every 10 minutes.

6. Transfer the contents to a serving dish and serve while hot.

BEEF CURRY

Serves 4.

Preparation and cooking time: 1 hr 40 mins.

This is a hot curry. It can be eaten on its own, but is usually served with boiled noodles, rice, chapattis, bread, puris, parothas, mashed potatoes, or pitta bread. For this recipe you need a liquidizer.

450g (1lb) shin or stewing beef
10g ($^1/_2$oz) fresh garlic, peeled
10g ($^1/_2$oz) fresh ginger, peeled
2 green chillies
55g (2oz) plum peeled tomatoes
30ml (1fl oz) cooking oil
1 large onion, finely chopped
$^1/_2$ tsp turmeric powder
1 tsp tomato purée
$^1/_2$ tsp chilli powder
1 tsp garam masala
1 tsp salt
1 tsp tandoori masala
4 tsp soy sauce
600ml (20fl oz) water
Small amount green dhanyia (coriander), chopped

Method

1.   Cut the beef into about 2.5cm (1 inch) cubes.
2.   Place the garlic, ginger, green chillies, and tomatoes into a liquidizer, and blend them into a thick paste.
3.   Heat the oil in a pan to a high temperature. Add the chopped onion and cook until it is golden brown. Add the beef cubes, blended paste, turmeric powder, tomato purée, chilli powder, garam masala, salt, tandoori masala, and soy sauce. Stir continuously for about 2 minutes. Reduce the heat, cover the pan and let it cook for about 20 minutes, stirring every few minutes. Add the water and stir. Simmer gently for a further hour.
4.   Transfer the curry into a serving dish, and garnish with the fresh dhanyia (coriander).

SPINACH LAMB

Serves 4.

Preparation and cooking time: 1 hr 10 mins.

Spinach is frequently used in Indian dishes, and spinach and lamb do make an excellent combination. This dish is quite mild, and can be served with chapattis, pitta bread, parothas or even bread. For this recipe you need a meat cleaver, or get your butcher to chop a leg of lamb up for you.

670g (1¹/₂lb) leg of lamb
340g (12oz) spinach
60ml (2fl oz) cooking oil
1 large onion, finely chopped
3 tsp tomato purée
1 tsp salt
1 tsp turmeric powder
¹/₂ tsp chilli powder
1 tsp garam masala
120ml (4fl oz) water

Method
1. Chop the leg of lamb into small pieces, about 2.5cm (1 inch) in length. There is no need to remove the bones.
2. Cut the spinach into small pieces and wash well.
3. Heat the oil to a high temperature in a large pan. Add the onion and cook until the onion is golden brown. Add the tomato purée, salt, turmeric powder, chilli powder and garam masala. Stir well and let the mixture cook for about 1 minute.
4. Add the lamb, spinach and the water. Mix well, lower the heat and simmer gently for about 40 minutes stirring every 5 to 7 minutes.
5. Transfer the contents to a serving dish and serve hot.
6. While eating, the bones are discarded and left on the plate.

MADRAS BUTTER BHOONA BEEF CURRY

Serves 4.

Preparation and cooking time: 1 hr 20 mins.

This is a medium dry beef curry, usually served with rice or chapattis.

450g (1lb) stewing beef
25g (1oz) butter
1 large onion, finely chopped
55g (2oz) plum peeled tomatoes, finely chopped
1 tsp tomato purée
1 tsp salt
1 tsp turmeric powder
1 tsp chilli powder
2 tsp madras curry powder
1 tsp garlic powder
450ml (15fl oz) water
Small amount green dhanyia (coriander), chopped

Method
1. Cut the beef into 2.5cm (1 inch) cubes.
2. Melt the butter in a large pan; add the onion and cook until golden brown, stirring continuously.
3. Add tomatoes, tomato purée, salt, turmeric powder, chilli powder, madras curry powder, garlic powder and the cubes of beef, and mix well. Stir continuously and cook for about 5 minutes.
4. Add the water, reduce the heat and simmer for about 1 hour stirring every 8 to 10 minutes.
5. Transfer the contents to a serving dish and garnish with the dhanyia (coriander).

FROZEN CHICKEN CURRY

Serves 4.

Preparation and cooking time: 1 hr 20 mins.

This is a mild to medium hot chicken curry. It is usually served with a rice dish, or chapattis. You can either use fresh green chillies (if you like curry dishes hot) or a fresh green pepper for milder taste. Parsley or coriander can be used for garnishing. For this recipe you need a liquidizer.

900g (2lb) frozen chicken pieces, thawed
25g (1oz) fresh garlic, peeled
25g (1oz) fresh ginger, peeled
3 green chillies or 1 green pepper, chopped (dependent on taste)
60ml (2fl oz) cooking oil
3 large onions, finely chopped
1 tsp turmeric powder
1 tsp chilli powder
2 tsp garam masala
1 tsp tandoori masala
3 tsp tomato purée
170g (6oz) plum peeled tomatoes
2 tsp salt
Parsley or green fresh dhanyia (coriander), chopped

Method

1. Remove the skin from the chicken pieces.
2. Place the garlic, ginger and green chillies (or green pepper) in a liquidizer and process until finely chopped.
3. Heat the oil to a high temperature in a pan. Add the chopped onions and cook until they are golden brown. Add the chicken pieces, the contents of the liquidizer, turmeric powder, chilli powder, garam masala, tandoori masala, tomato purée, tomatoes and salt. Stir continuously for a few minutes.
4. Reduce the heat and simmer for about 1 hour, stirring every 5 to 7 minutes, keeping the pan covered all the time.
5. Garnish with chopped parsley or fresh dhanyia (coriander).
6. The bones are discarded while eating and left on the plate.

FRESH CHICKEN CURRY

Serves 4.

Preparation and cooking time: 1 hr 50 mins.

This is a very popular curry, usually served with rice or chapattis. It takes longer to cook than the frozen chicken curry, and tastes quite different.

60ml (2fl oz) cooking oil
2 large onions, finely chopped
900g (2lb) fresh chicken, skinned and cut into small pieces
8oz (225g) plum peeled tomatoes
1 tsp salt
1 tsp chilli powder
1 tsp turmeric powder
2 tsp garam masala
1 tsp garlic powder
1 tsp ginger powder
3 green chillies, finely chopped
600ml (20fl oz) water
Small amount green dhanyia (coriander), chopped

Method

1. Heat the oil in a large pan to a high temperature. Add the onions and cook until they are golden brown.

2. Add the chicken, tomatoes, salt, chilli powder, turmeric powder, garam masala, garlic powder, ginger powder and the green chillies. Stir continuously for about 5 minutes.

3. Cover the pan, reduce the heat and simmer gently for about 25 minutes.

4. Add half of the water (300ml/10fl oz) to the curry and bring the mixture to the boil. Reduce the heat, cover the pan, and cook for a further 35 minutes, stirring every 10 minutes. Add the remaining water, and simmer for a further 45 minutes, stirring every 15 minutes.

5. Transfer the contents to a serving dish, and garnish with the dhanyia (coriander). Serve while hot.

6. The bones are discarded while eating and left on the plate.

FRIED CHICKEN CURRY

Serves 4.

Preparation and cooking time: 1 hr 20 mins.

This is a mouth-watering chicken curry, and is fairly simple to cook. It is usually served with chapattis, rice, noodles or even with chips or mashed potatoes. For this recipe you need either a meat cleaver or a very sharp knife, and a wok or deep frying pan.

900g (2lb) chicken pieces
600ml (20fl oz) cooking oil, for deep frying
60ml (2fl oz) cooking oil
3 large onions, finely chopped
1 tsp chilli powder
1 tsp garam masala
6 green chillies, finely chopped
1 tsp garlic powder
2 tsp tandoori masala
1 tsp turmeric powder
1 tsp salt
4 tsp soy sauce
2 tsp tomato purée
300ml (10fl oz) water
Small amount green dhanyia (coriander), chopped

Method

1. Remove the skin from the chicken pieces, and chop the chicken into smaller pieces, about 7cm (3 inches) long. The bones are left in the chicken pieces.

2. Heat the 600ml (20fl oz) of cooking oil in a wok or deep frying pan to a high temperature. Deep fry all the chicken pieces, about 4 to 5 at a time, until they are golden brown.

3. Heat the 60ml (2fl oz) of oil in another pan and fry the chopped onions until they are golden brown. Add the chilli powder, garam masala, green chillies, garlic powder, tandoori masala, turmeric powder, salt, soy sauce, and tomato purée. Mix well and cook for about 1 to 2 minutes.

4. Add the fried chicken, mix well and cook for a further 2 to 3 minutes, stirring continuously. Add the water, stir, and bring the mixture to the boil. Reduce the heat, cover the pan and simmer gently for a further 15 minutes.

5. Transfer the curry to a serving dish and garnish with the green dhanyia (coriander).

6. The bones are discarded while eating and left on the plate.

PORK CURRY

Serves 4.

Preparation and cooking time: 1 hr 10 mins.

This is a dry hot curry. It can be eaten as a snack on its own, or served with mashed potatoes, chapattis, pitta bread or parothas. For this recipe you need a liquidizer.

900g (2lb) boneless pork
10g ($^1/_2$oz) fresh garlic, peeled
10g ($^1/_2$oz) fresh ginger, peeled
2 green chillies
225g (8oz) fresh tomatoes
30ml (1fl oz) cooking oil
1 large onion, finely chopped
$^1/_2$ tsp turmeric powder
$^1/_2$ tsp chilli powder
$^1/_2$ tsp tandoori masala
1 tsp salt
1 tsp garam masala
120ml (4fl oz) water
Small amount green dhanyia (coriander), chopped

Method

1. Cut the pork pieces into about 2.5cm (1 inch) cubes.
2. Blend the garlic, ginger and green chillies in a liquidizer until finely chopped.
3. Cut the tomatoes into small pieces.
4. Heat the oil in a pan to a high temperature; add the chopped onion and cook until it is golden brown.
5. Add the contents of the liquidizer, tomatoes, pork cubes, turmeric powder, chilli powder, tandoori masala, salt and garam masala. Stir continuously for about 2 minutes.
6. Reduce the heat, cover the pan and simmer gently for about 20 minutes, stirring every 5 to 7 minutes.
7. Add the water, stir and simmer gently for a further 30 minutes, again stirring every 5 to 7 minutes.
8. Transfer the curry to a serving dish. Garnish with fresh green dhanyia (coriander) and serve while hot.

STUFFED MACKEREL CURRY

Serves 4.

Preparation and cooking time: 8 hrs 30 mins.

Spiced and stuffed mackerel is tasty and makes a good change from meat curries. It is usually served with fried rice and can be served with salad as a starter. For this recipe you need a liquidizer.

25g (1oz) fresh garlic, peeled
25g (1oz) fresh ginger, peeled
6 green chillies
2 tsp tomato purée
30ml (1fl oz) yoghurt
$^1/_2$ tsp salt
$^1/_2$ tsp turmeric powder
$^1/_2$ tsp dhanyia powder (coriander)
$^1/_2$ tsp jeera powder (cumin)
1 tsp lemon juice
4 small fresh mackerel – about 450g (1lb) in total
60ml (2fl oz) cooking oil
Small amount green dhanyia (coriander), chopped

Method

1. Place the garlic, ginger, chillies, tomato purée, yoghurt, salt, turmeric powder, dhanyia powder, jeera powder, and lemon juice in a liquidizer and blend into a thickish paste.

2. Cut the heads off the mackerel and slice the fish along their tops, on one side only, so as to enable you to remove the bones from their centres. Make sure that you do not cut completely through, and the mackerel are still whole.

3. Place the mackerel under cold running water for about one minute.

4. Carefully lay the four mackerel out in a large pan and pour the thick paste in the space left by the bones of each of the mackerel. Lift the other half and fold it back so that the blended liquid is in the middle of each of the mackerel.

5. Now leave the fish for about 8 hours.

6. Heat the oil to a high temperature, in a large flat pan. Transfer the fish very carefully to this pan with the hot oil, lower the heat and let it simmer for about 5 minutes. While simmering cover the pan. Turn the fish over carefully, still folded, and cook the other sides by simmering for a further 5 minutes.

7. Transfer the contents to a serving dish and garnish with the dhanyia (coriander). Serve while hot.

COD FISH CURRY

Serves 4.

Preparation and cooking time: 40 mins.

Cod curry is unusual but makes an excellent alternative to meat curries. It can be served with mashed potatoes, chapattis or fried rice. For this recipe you need a liquidizer.

10g (^{1}/$_2$oz) fresh garlic, peeled
10g (^{1}/$_2$oz) fresh ginger, peeled
1 green chilli
225g (8oz) plum peeled tomatoes
60ml (2fl oz) cooking oil
1 large onion, finely chopped
^{1}/$_2$ tsp turmeric powder
^{1}/$_2$ tsp chilli powder
^{1}/$_2$ tsp garam masala
^{1}/$_2$ tsp salt
670g (1^1/$_2$lb) cod steaks
Small amount green dhanyia (coriander), chopped

Method

1. Blend the garlic, ginger, chilli and tomatoes in a liquidizer, to a thickish paste.

2. Heat the oil to a high temperature in a pan; add the onion and cook until it is golden brown.

3. Add the contents of the liquidizer, turmeric powder, chilli powder, garam masala and salt, and stir continuously for about 2 minutes. Cook this mixture for a further 3 minutes.

4. Arrange the fish steaks in a large casserole and spread the spiced mixture on top of the steaks.

5. Bake the fish and the mixture in a pre-heated oven at mark 4 (350°F or 180°C), for about 20 minutes.

6. Garnish the fish with fresh green dhanyia (coriander) and serve hot.

DRY BHOONA MUSHROOM AND PRAWN CURRY

Serves 4.

Preparation and cooking time: 20 mins.

This is a very mild prawn curry usually served as a side dish with meat curry. For this recipe you need a liquidizer.

10g ($^1/_2$ oz) fresh garlic
10g ($^1/_2$ oz) fresh ginger
4 green chillies
60ml (2fl oz) cooking oil
1 large onion, finely chopped
1 tsp tomato purée
$^1/_2$ tsp salt
$^1/_2$ tsp turmeric powder
$^1/_2$ tsp chilli powder
$^1/_2$ tsp dhanyia powder (coriander)
$^1/_2$ tsp jeera powder (cumin)
225g (8oz) mushrooms, cut into halves
110g (4oz) peeled prawns
Small amount green dhanyia (coriander), chopped
2 oz (55g) fresh tomatoes, cut into rings

Method

1. Place the garlic, ginger and green chillies in a liquidizer, and chop finely.
2. Heat the oil to a high temperature, in a pan. Add the onion, stir continuously and cook until golden brown. Add the contents of the liquidizer, tomato purée, salt, turmeric powder, chilli powder, dhanyia powder and jeera powder. Cook the mixture for a further minute, stirring continuously.
3. Add the mushrooms and prawns. Mix well, lower the heat, cover the pan and simmer gently for about 8 minutes, stirring every 2 to 3 minutes.
4. Transfer the contents to a serving dish and garnish with the green dhanyia and tomatoes.

EGG AND POTATO CURRY

Serves 4.

Preparation and cooking time: 45 mins.

This is a mild curry not usually served in restaurants. It can be served with rice or chapattis.

6 eggs
225g (8oz) potatoes
30ml (1fl oz) cooking oil
1 onion, finely chopped
110g (4oz) plum peeled tomatoes
1 tsp salt
1 tsp turmeric powder
1 tsp garam masala
$^1/_2$ tsp chilli powder
$^1/_2$ tsp tandoori masala
1 tsp cumin powder
150ml (5fl oz) water
Small amount green dhanyia (coriander), chopped

Method

1. Hard boil the eggs and remove the shells. Cut the eggs into halves.
2. Peel the potatoes and cut into small pieces, about 1cm ($^1/_2$ inch) cubes.
3. Heat the oil to a high temperature in a pan. Add the onion and cook until the onion is golden brown, stirring continuously.
4. Add the tomatoes and cook for about a further 2 minutes stirring continuously. Now add the salt, turmeric powder, garam masala, chilli powder, tandoori masala and cumin powder. Cook for a further 1 minute.
5. Add the potatoes, mix well, and cook for about 2 minutes stirring continuously. Now add the eggs and cook for about 3 to 4 minutes.
6. Add the water; bring it to the boil; lower the heat and let it simmer for about 20 minutes, stirring every 5 to 7 minutes.
7. Transfer the contents to a serving dish and garnish with the coriander.

PRAWN AND PEPPER CURRY

Serves 4.

Preparation and cooking time: 25 mins.

Prawns are rare in Indian homes, but prawn curries do taste good, and are always worth a try. For this recipe you need a deep frying pan or wok.

340g (12oz) green peppers
60ml (2fl oz) cooking oil
2 medium size onions, finely chopped
2 ripe tomatoes cut into small pieces
1 tsp salt
$^1/_2$ tsp turmeric powder
$^1/_2$ tsp chilli powder
$^1/_2$ tsp garam masala
340g (12oz) peeled prawns

Method
1. Chop the peppers lengthways into pieces about 2.5cm (1 inch) long and 1cm ($^1/_2$ inch) wide.
2. Heat the oil in a large wok, add the onions and fry them until they are golden brown. Add the tomatoes, salt, turmeric powder, chilli powder and garam masala. Cook for a further 2 minutes.
3. Add the peppers and prawns and stir well. Reduce the heat, cover the wok and cook on a very low heat for a further 15 minutes, stirring every 3 to 4 minutes.
4. Transfer the contents to a serving dish and serve hot.

4
DHALS

VALL DHAL

Serves 4.

Preparation and cooking time: 2 hrs 40 mins.

This is a dhal curry usually served with chapattis, bread, rice or pitta bread.

225g (8oz) vall dhal
900ml (30fl oz) water
30ml (1fl oz) cooking oil
$^1/_2$ tsp whole jeera (cumin seeds)
$^1/_2$ tsp whole rai (black mustard seeds)
$^1/_4$ tsp hing (asafoetida)
2 tsp tomato purée
1 tsp turmeric powder
1 tsp chilli powder
1 tsp garlic powder
1 tsp ginger powder
1 tsp salt
1 tsp garam masala
Small amount green dhanyia (coriander), chopped

Method

1. Wash the vall dhal as described in the introduction (page 16). Then leave the dhal to soak in the 900ml (30fl oz) of water for 2 hours.
2. Heat the oil to a high temperature, in a pan. Add the jeera to the hot oil, and then a few seconds later add the rai and asafoetida. Leave for a few more seconds and add the tomato purée, turmeric powder, chilli powder, garlic powder, ginger powder, salt and garam masala. Cook for a further 2 minutes, stirring continuously.
3. Drain the dhal, and save the water in which it was soaking, in another pan. Add the dhal to the spiced mixture. Cook for a further 2 minutes, stirring continuously.
4. Add the water in which the dhal was soaked to the above mixture. Bring the water to the boil and simmer gently for a further 30 minutes, stirring every 5 minutes.
5. Place the dhal in a serving dish and garnish with fresh dhanyia (coriander).

SPLIT URAD DHAL

Serves 4.

Preparation and cooking time: 1 hr 25 mins.

This dhal curry is usually served with chapattis or bread. It can also be served with hot pitta bread. It is very popular with vegetarians. Green chillies can be used if you like hot curries, but otherwise a pepper can be used for a milder taste. For this recipe you need a liquidizer.

170g (6oz) skinless split urad dhal
1 large onion, finely chopped
1200ml (40fl oz) water
1 tsp salt
85g (3oz) plum peeled tomatoes
3 green chillies or 1 green pepper, chopped
25g (1oz) fresh garlic, peeled
25g (1oz) fresh ginger, peeled
60ml (2fl oz) cooking oil
$^1/_2$ tsp whole jeera (cumin seeds)
$^1/_2$ tsp whole rai (black mustard seeds)
1 tsp turmeric powder
1 tsp chilli powder
1 tsp garam masala
Small amount green dhanyia (coriander), chopped

Method

1. Wash the dhal as described in the introduction (page 16).
2. Place the washed dhal, chopped onion and the 1200ml (40fl oz) of water in a large pan.
3. Add the salt.
4. Bring the water to the boil, reduce the heat, and simmer gently for about 1 hour, stirring every 5 to 7 minutes.
5. Place the tomatoes, green chillies, garlic and ginger in a liquidizer and blend into a thickish paste.
6. Heat the oil to a high temperature, in a separate pan. Add the jeera and rai and let it cook for a few seconds. Add the contents of the liquidizer, turmeric powder, chilli powder and garam masala. Stir continuously and cook for 2 to 3 minutes.
7. Add this spicy mixture to the boiled dhal, and boil for another 5 minutes.
8. Place the dhal in a serving dish and garnish with fresh dhanyia (coriander).

RED KIDNEY BEANS (WHOLE) DHAL

Serves 4.

Preparation and cooking time: 2 hrs 20 mins.

This is a very popular curry all over India. It is usually served with chapattis, bread, pitta bread, puris, parothas, or simply rice. If you like sweet and sour dishes then sugar can be added to give it a slightly sweeter taste. This makes it very versatile. For this recipe you need a liquidizer.

NB Red kidney beans must be boiled for at least 1 hour as indicated in this recipe, otherwise they could be poisonous.

170g (6oz) red kidney beans
1200ml (40fl oz) water
1 tsp salt
55g (2oz) plum peeled tomatoes
2 green chillies
25g (1oz) fresh garlic, peeled
60ml (2fl oz) cooking oil
$^1/_2$ tsp whole jeera (cumin seeds)
$^1/_2$ tsp whole rai (black mustard seeds)
1 large onion, finely chopped
1 tsp tandoori masala
1 tsp turmeric powder
1 tsp garam masala
1 tsp sugar (optional)
30ml (1fl oz) lemon juice
1 tsp tomato purée
$^1/_2$ tsp chilli powder
Small amount green dhanyia (coriander), chopped

Method

1. Boil the beans in the 1200ml (40fl oz) of salted water for about 1 hour and 15 minutes. This will make the beans soft, and this can be tested by being able to pulp the bean easily, with your fingers.

2. Place the tomatoes, green chillies, and garlic in a liquidizer, and blend to a thickish paste.

3. Heat the oil to a high temperature in a large pan. Add the whole jeera and rai and cook for a few seconds. Add the onion and cook until it is golden brown.

4. Add the contents of the liquidizer, tandoori masala, turmeric powder, garam masala, sugar (if required), lemon juice, tomato purée and chilli powder. Cook together for a further 1 minute.

5. Add the beans with the water. Lower the heat, and simmer gently for a further 30 minutes, stirring every 5 to 7 minutes.

6. Transfer the contents to a serving dish and garnish with fresh dhanyia (coriander). Serve hot.

WHOLE URAD AND
RED KIDNEY BEANS DHAL

Serves 4.

Preparation and cooking time: 2 hrs 40 mins.

This is a rather mild dhal. Like all dhals, it is usually served with boiled rice or chapattis but can be served with bread. If you like hot curries then green chillies should be used, but otherwise a green pepper can be used instead.

NB The urad and red kidney beans must be boiled for at least 2 hours as indicated in the recipe, otherwise the beans are poisonous.

85g (3oz) whole urad
25g (1oz) red kidney beans
1800ml (60fl oz) water
1 large onion, finely chopped
2 green chillies, finely chopped, or 1 green pepper, finely chopped
1 tsp salt
30ml (1fl oz) cooking oil
$^1/_2$ tsp whole jeera (cumin seeds)
2 tsp tomato purée
$^1/_2$ tsp turmeric powder
1 tsp chilli powder
1 tsp garam masala
Some fresh green dhanyia (coriander), finely chopped

Method

1. Mix the urad and red kidney beans. Wash the beans and urad as described in the introduction (page 16).
2. Place the washed, mixed dhal in the 1800ml (60fl oz) of water.
3. Add the chopped onion, the chopped chillies (or green pepper), and the salt, and bring to the boil.
4. Reduce the heat, cover the pan and boil gently, stirring every 15 minutes, until the consistency is like thin porridge. This usually takes about two and a half hours.
5. Heat the oil to a high temperature, in a separate pan. Add the jeera, tomato purée, turmeric powder, chilli powder, and garam masala. Stir continuously and simmer the mixture for about 1 minute. Add the mixture to the dhal and simmer the dhal gently for another 3 to 5 minutes.
6. Transfer the cooked dhal to a serving dish and garnish with the fresh dhanyia (coriander).

SPLIT MOONG AND SPLIT LENTIL DHAL

Serves 4.

Preparation and cooking time: 45 mins.

This is a mixed dhal, usually served with chapattis, bread, puris (deep fried chapattis – see recipe on 186), parothas, rice or pitta bread. It can also be used like a soup, as a starter. It is very popular with vegetarians.

85g (3oz) skinless, split moong dhal
85g (3oz) skinless, split lentil dhal
900ml (30fl oz) water
1 large onion, finely chopped
1 tsp salt
60ml (2fl oz) cooking oil
$^1/_2$ tsp whole jeera (cumin seeds)
$^1/_2$ tsp whole rai (black mustard seeds)
2 tsp tomato purée
1 tsp turmeric powder
1 tsp garam masala
6 bay leaves
1 tsp chilli powder
Small amount green dhanyia (coriander), chopped

Method

1. Mix the moong and lentil dhals. Wash the dhal as described in the introduction (page 16).
2. Place the washed dhal, the chopped onion and the 900ml (30fl oz) of water in a large pan and add the salt.
3. Bring the water to the boil, reduce the heat and simmer gently for about 30 minutes, stirring every 5 to 7 minutes.
4. Heat the oil to a high temperature in a separate pan. Add the jeera and rai and leave it to cook for a few seconds. Add the tomato purée, turmeric powder, garam masala, bay leaves and chilli powder. Stir continuously and cook for a few seconds. Pour the boiled dhal into the mixture, and simmer for a further 5 minutes.
5. Transfer the dhal to a serving dish and garnish with fresh dhanyia (coriander).
6. The bay leaves are discarded and left on the plate, while eating.

WHOLE LENTIL DHAL

Serves 4.

Preparation and cooking time: 55 mins.

This is a rather mild dhal. It is usually served with boiled rice, chapattis or bread. Chilli powder can be used for making a hot dhal, otherwise paprika powder can be used for a milder taste. Fresh parsley or green fresh coriander can be used for garnishing.

170g (6oz) whole lentils
900ml (30fl oz) water
1$^{1}/_{2}$ tsp salt
60ml (2fl oz) cooking oil
$^{1}/_{2}$ tsp whole jeera (cumin seeds)
1 large onion, finely chopped
2 tsp tomato purée
1 tsp turmeric powder
1 tsp chilli powder, or paprika powder for mild taste
2 tsp garam masala
1 tsp tandoori masala
Some fresh parsley or green fresh dhanyia (coriander), finely
    chopped

Method

1. Wash the whole lentils, as described in the introduction (page 16).
2. Place the washed lentils in the 900ml (30fl oz) of water, add the salt and bring to the boil.
3. Reduce the heat, cover the pan and simmer gently for about 45 minutes, stirring every 5 to 7 minutes.
4. Heat the oil to a high temperature in a separate pan. When it is hot, add the jeera and the chopped onion. Cook together until the onion is golden brown. Add the tomato purée, turmeric powder, chilli powder (or paprika powder), garam masala and tandoori masala. Stir continuously and simmer the mixture for about 1 minute.
5. Add the spiced mixture to the cooked lentil dhal.
6. Simmer gently for about 3 to 5 minutes. Transfer the contents to a serving dish and garnish with the dhanyia or parsley.

SPLIT LENTIL DHAL

Serves 4.

Preparation and cooking time: 40 mins.

This dhal tastes very different from whole lentil and is usually served with plain boiled rice, or sometimes like soup, as a starter.

170g (6oz) skinless split lentils
1200ml (40fl oz) water
1 large onion, finely chopped
1 tsp salt
60ml (2fl oz) cooking oil
$^1/_2$ tsp whole jeera (cumin seeds)
$^1/_2$ tsp whole rai (black mustard seeds)
55g (2oz) plum peeled tomatoes
1 tsp turmeric powder
$^1/_2$ tsp garam masala
$^1/_2$ tsp chilli powder
Small amount green dhanyia (coriander), chopped

Method

1. Wash the dhal as described in the introduction (page 16).
2. Place the dhal, the 1200ml (40fl oz) of water and the chopped onion in a large pan. Add the salt and stir well.
3. Bring the water to the boil, reduce the heat and simmer gently for about 30 minutes, stirring every 5 to 7 minutes. This boiled dhal can be served as soup if desired.
4. Heat the oil to a high temperature in a separate pan or wok. Add the jeera and rai and leave it to cook for a few seconds. Add the tomatoes, turmeric powder, garam masala, and chilli powder. Stir continuously and cook until the tomatoes have reduced to a pulp. This will usually take about 2 to 3 minutes.
5. Add the boiled dhal to this spice mixture, reduce the heat and simmer gently for a further 5 minutes.
6. Transfer the contents to a serving dish and garnish with the fresh green dhanyia (coriander). Serve hot.

WHOLE MOONG, DRY

Serves 4.

Preparation and cooking time: 10 hrs 30 mins.

This is one of the many dhal curries usually served with chapattis. It also makes a good filling for toasted sandwiches. It may also be served with rice and a meat curry dish.

170g (6oz) whole moong
1200ml (40fl oz) water for soaking moong
60ml (2fl oz) cooking oil
$^1/_2$ tsp whole jeera (cumin seeds)
$^1/_2$ tsp whole rai (black mustard seeds)
1 tsp turmeric powder
1 tsp garam masala
1 tsp chilli powder
2 tsp tomato purée
1 tsp salt
4 tsp soy sauce
450ml (15fl oz) water for cooking
Small amount green dhanyia (coriander), chopped

Method

1. Soak the moong overnight in the 1200ml (40fl oz) of water.
2. Wash the whole moong as described in the introduction (page 16).
3. Heat the oil to a high temperature in a separate pan. Add the jeera and rai, and leave it to cook for a few seconds. Add the washed moong, turmeric powder, garam masala, chilli powder, tomato purée, salt and soy sauce. Stir continuously and cook for about 3 minutes. Add the 450ml (15fl oz) of water and bring it to the boil.
4. Reduce the heat, cover the pan and simmer gently for about 30 minutes, stirring every 5 to 7 minutes.
5. Transfer the contents to a serving dish and garnish with fresh green dhanyia (coriander).

TOOVAR DHAL

Serves 4.

Preparation and cooking time: 40 mins.

This is one of the popular dhals of southern India, and has a sweet and sour taste. It is usually served with chapattis, bread, puris (deep fried chapattis – see recipe on page 186), parothas or rice. It is a dish which pleases vegetarians. For this recipe you need a pressure cooker.

170g (6oz) toovar dhal
900ml (30fl oz) water
1 tsp salt
60ml (2fl oz) cooking oil
$^1/_2$ tsp whole jeera (cumin seeds)
$^1/_2$ tsp whole rai (black mustard seeds)
4 whole cloves
4 whole black peppercorns
$^1/_4$ tsp hing (asafoetida)
1 tsp tomato purée
1 tsp turmeric powder
6 bay leaves
1 tsp chilli powder
2 green chillies, sliced into halves
$^1/_2$ tsp sugar
10g ($^1/_2$oz) peanuts
15ml ($^1/_2$fl oz) lemon juice
Small amount green dhanyia (coriander), chopped

Method

1. Wash the dhal as described in the introduction (page 16).

2. Place the washed dhal in a pressure cooker, add the 900ml (30fl oz) of water and salt, and cook on high pressure for about 15 minutes after the initial boil whistle. Switch off the heat, but leave the dhal cooking in the pressure cooker.

3. Heat the oil to a high temperature in a separate pan and add the jeera, rai, cloves, peppercorns, and asafoetida. Cook for a few seconds. Add the tomato purée, turmeric powder, bay leaves, chilli powder, green chillies, sugar, peanuts, and lemon juice. Stir continuously for a few seconds. Pour the boiled dhal into the mixture and simmer gently together for a further 10 minutes, stirring every 2 minutes.

4. Transfer the dhal into a serving dish and garnish with the dhanyia (coriander). Serve hot.

5. The bay leaves and peppercorns are discarded and left on the plate while eating.

BLACK CHANA DHAL

Serves 4.

Preparation and cooking time: 11 hrs 20 mins.

Black chana are more common in southern India than in the north, and taste somewhat like chick peas. They are not usually served in restaurants, and therefore are worth trying at home.

340g (12oz) black chana
900ml (30fl oz) water for soaking the chana
900ml (30fl oz) water for boiling the chana
1 tsp salt
60ml (2fl oz) cooking oil
$^1/_2$ tsp whole jeera (cumin seeds)
$^1/_4$ tsp hing (asafoetida)
$^1/_2$ tsp whole rai (black mustard seeds)
2 tsp tomato purée
$^1/_2$ tsp chilli powder
1 tsp tandoori masala
$^1/_2$ tsp turmeric powder
4 green chillies, finely chopped
1 tsp garam masala
30ml (1fl oz) lemon juice
450ml (15fl oz) water for cooking
Small amount green dhanyia (coriander), chopped

Method

1. Wash the chana as described in the introduction (page 16).
2. Soak the chana overnight in the 900ml (30fl oz) of water.
3. Next day, drain the water. Add the fresh 900ml (30fl oz) of water and the salt and bring the mixture to the boil. Reduce the heat, cover the pan and simmer gently for about 1 hour.
4. Heat the oil to a high temperature in a separate pan or wok. Add the jeera, asafoetida, and the rai. Cook for a few seconds. Add the tomato purée, chilli powder, tandoori masala, turmeric powder, green chillies, garam masala and lemon juice. Stir well and cook for a further few seconds.
5. Now add the chana and the 450ml (15fl oz) of water for cooking. Bring the water to the boil; lower the heat and then simmer gently for a further 15 minutes.
6. Transfer the contents to a serving dish and garnish with fresh green dhanyia (coriander).

WHITE CHANA DHAL

Serves 4.

Preparation and cooking time: 11 hrs 40 mins.

White chana curry is a traditional dish in the Punjab and northern parts of India. It is a very special dish for dinner parties, wedding parties, picnics, etc. It is usually served with bhaturas, puris, chapattis, or even pitta bread. It also makes a good filling for toasted sandwiches.

340g (12oz) white chana
900ml (30fl oz) water for soaking chana
900ml (30fl oz) water for boiling chana
1 tsp salt
60ml (2fl oz) cooking oil
$^1/_2$ tsp whole jeera (cumin seeds)
$^1/_2$ tsp whole rai (black mustard seeds)
2 large onions, finely chopped
3 green chillies, finely chopped
2 tsp tomato purée
$^1/_2$ tsp chilli powder
$1^1/_2$ tsp tandoori masala
1 tsp turmeric powder
$^1/_2$ tsp garlic powder
$1^1/_2$ tsp garam masala
30ml (1fl oz) lemon juice

For garnishing
Small tomato, cut into rings
1 onion, cut into small rings
Small amount green dhanyia (coriander), chopped

Method

1. Wash the chana as described in the introduction (page 16).
2. Soak the chana overnight in the 900ml (30fl oz) of water.
3. Next day, drain the water. Place the chana in a large cooking pot, add the fresh 900ml (30fl oz) water and the salt, and bring the mixture to the boil. Reduce the heat, cover the pan and simmer gently for about 1 hour.
4. In a separate pan, heat the oil to a high temperature. Add the jeera and rai; cook for a few seconds until they are slightly brown. Add the onions and green chillies, and cook until the onions are golden brown. Add the tomato purée, chilli powder, tandoori masala, turmeric powder, garlic powder, garam masala and lemon juice. Stir continuously and cook for a further 2 minutes.
5. Drain the chana, but save the water. Add the drained chana to the spice mixture. Cook for a further 2 minutes, stirring continuously. Add the water which was drained from the chana, reduce the heat, cover the pan and simmer for about 5 minutes.
6. Place the cooked chana in a serving dish and garnish with tomatoes, onion and dhanyia. Serve while hot, or allow to cool and use as filling for toasted sandwiches.

BLACK EYE BEANS DHAL

Serves 4.

Preparation and cooking time: 11 hrs.

Black eye beans taste similar to chick peas, and are usually served with rice.

NB The beans must be cooked for at least 20 minutes, otherwise they could cause indigestion.

225g (8oz) black eye beans
900ml (30fl oz) water for soaking
60ml (2fl oz) cooking oil
$^1/_2$ tsp whole jeera (cumin seeds)
$^1/_2$ tsp whole rai (black mustard seeds)
1 tsp salt
1 tsp turmeric powder
1 tsp chilli powder
1 tsp dhanyia powder (coriander)
1 tsp jeera powder (cumin)
2 tsp tomato purée
600ml (20fl oz) water for cooking
Small amount of dhanyia (coriander)

Method

1. Soak the beans overnight in the 900ml (30fl oz) of water.
2. Wash the beans as described in the introduction (page 16).
3. Heat the oil to a high temperature in a large pan. Add the jeera and rai and let it cook for a few seconds. Add the washed beans, salt, turmeric powder, chilli powder, dhanyia powder, jeera powder and tomato purée. Mix well and cook for about 2 minutes stirring continuously.
4. Add the 600ml (20fl oz) of water, bring to the boil, lower the heat, cover the pan and simmer for about 25 minutes, stirring every 5 to 7 minutes.
5. Transfer the contents to a serving dish and garnish with the dhanyia. Serve while hot.

CHANA AND MARROW DHAL

Serves 4.

Preparation and cooking time: 1 hr 20 mins.

Dhals are sometimes cooked mixed with other dhals or vegetables. Marrow makes a very good addition to the chana dhal and is well worth a try. For this recipe you need a pressure cooker.

110g (4oz) chana dhal
225g (8oz) marrow, peeled and diced into small cubes
900ml (30fl oz) water
1 tsp salt
60ml (2fl oz) cooking oil
110g (4oz) onions, finely chopped
85g (3oz) tomatoes, finely chopped
1 tsp turmeric powder
1 tsp chilli powder
1 tsp garam masala
3 green chillies, finely chopped
2 tsp lemon juice
Small amount green dhanyia (coriander), chopped

Method

1. Wash the dhal as described in the introduction (page 16).
2. Place the washed dhal and marrow in a pressure cooker. Add the water and salt, cover the lid and cook for about 30 minutes on high pressure. Switch off the heat after this time but leave the dhal cooking in the pressure cooker for another 30 minutes.
3. Heat the oil to a high temperature in another pan. Add the onions and cook them until they are golden brown. Add the tomatoes, turmeric powder, chilli powder, garam masala, green chillies and the lemon juice. Cook this spice mixture for about another 2 minutes.
4. Add the spice mixture to the dhal, stir well and cook together for about 5 minutes, stirring every 2 to 3 minutes.
5. Transfer the dhal to a serving dish and garnish with the dhanyia. Serve hot.

SPLIT MOONG DHAL

Serves 4.

Preparation and cooking time: 40 mins.

This is one of the many dhal curries usually served with chapattis, bread or rice. Like most dhals it is popular with vegetarians.

170g (6oz) skinless split moong dhal
1 tsp salt
1 large onion, finely chopped
900ml (30fl oz) water
60ml (2fl oz) cooking oil
$^1/_2$ tsp whole jeera (cumin seeds)
$^1/_2$ tsp whole rai (black mustard seeds)
25g (1oz) fresh garlic, peeled and finely chopped
85g (3oz) plum peeled tomatoes
1 tsp turmeric powder
1 tsp garam masala
1 tsp chilli powder
Small amount green dhanyia (coriander), chopped

Method
1. Wash the dhal as described in the introduction (page 16).
2. Add the salt, chopped onion and the water to the washed dhal. Boil the water, lower the heat and simmer gently for about 30 minutes stirring every 5 to 7 minutes.
3. Heat the oil to a high temperature, in a separate pan and add the jeera, rai and chopped garlic. Cook for a few seconds. Add the tomatoes, turmeric powder, garam masala and chilli powder and cook for a further 3 to 4 minutes, stirring continuously.
4. Add this spice mixture to the boiled dhal, and simmer gently for a further 5 to 7 minutes.
5. Transfer the dhal to a serving dish and garnish with the fresh green dhanyia (coriander).

5

VEGETABLE CURRIES

CUT OKRA CURRY

Serves 4.

Preparation and cooking time: 45 mins.

Okra, also sometimes called ladies' fingers, is a very popular vegetable in India. Like most vegetable curries, this is usually served with dhal and rice, or meat curry and rice. It may also be served with chapattis alone. For this recipe you need a liquidizer.

25g (1oz) fresh garlic, peeled
2 green chillies
55g (2oz) fresh ginger, peeled
340g (12oz) fresh okra
90ml (3fl oz) cooking oil
340g (12oz) onions, chopped into large pieces
2 tsp tomato purée
1 tsp salt
$^1/_2$ tsp chilli powder
$^1/_2$ tsp turmeric powder
1 tsp garam masala
1 fresh tomato, cut into small pieces, for garnish

Method

1. Place the garlic, green chillies, and ginger into a liquidizer and chop finely.
2. Wash the okra and then dry each piece individually with kitchen roll paper. This is very important as okra should be as dry as possible.
3. Cut the okra into 1cm ($^1/_2$ inch) long pieces, lengthways.
4. Heat the oil to a high temperature in a pan, add the contents of the liquidizer, and cook for a few seconds. Add the onions and cook together, stirring continuously, until the onions are very light brown. Add the tomato purée, salt, chilli powder, turmeric powder, and garam masala. Cook for a few seconds, and add the okra. Stir continuously for 2 to 3 minutes.
5. Reduce the heat, cover the pan and simmer gently for about 25 minutes. The heat must be kept very low, and the mixture needs to be stirred every 5 to 7 minutes.
6. Transfer the okra curry into a serving dish and garnish with the fresh tomato pieces.

OKRA AND CHIPS CURRY

Serves 4.

Preparation and cooking time: 25 mins.

Okra, or ladies' fingers, is a very popular vegetable in Indian homes, and since most people like potatoes, okra and chips make an attractive combination.

225g (8oz) fresh okra
60ml (2fl oz) cooking oil
3 large onions, finely chopped
1/2 tsp salt
1/2 tsp turmeric powder
1/2 tsp chilli powder
1/2 tsp garam masala
1/2 tsp tomato purée
110g (4oz) fried potato chips
1 fresh tomato, cut into small pieces

Method

1. Wash the okra and then dry each piece individually with kitchen roll paper. This is extremely important as okra must be as dry as possible.
2. Cut the okra into 1cm ($^1/_2$ inch) long pieces lengthways.
3. Heat the oil to a high temperature in a wok or deep frying pan. Add the onions and the okra. Stir, reduce the heat, cover the pan and let the okra and onions cook for about 10 minutes, stirring every 3 to 4 minutes.
4. Now add the salt, turmeric powder, chilli powder, garam masala and tomato purée. Mix well and let it cook for a further 3 to 4 minutes.
5. Add the chips, mix well and let it cook for another 3 to 4 minutes.
6. Transfer the contents to a serving dish and garnish with the tomato.

FROZEN MIXED VEGETABLE CURRY

Serves 4.

Preparation and cooking time: 30 mins.

If you are in a hurry, then this curry is ideal. It does not take too long to cook, and can be served with plain boiled rice. It is also good served with bread, or chapattis.

45ml (1½fl oz) cooking oil
½ tsp whole jeera (cumin seeds)
½ tsp whole rai (black mustard seeds)
1 large onion, finely chopped
2 tsp tomato purée
1 tsp turmeric powder
1 tsp chilli powder
1 tsp garam masala
1 tsp salt
1 tsp garlic powder
450g (1lb) frozen, mixed vegetables
2 small potatoes, chopped into very small pieces
300ml (10fl oz) water

Method
1. Heat the oil to a high temperature in a pan, and add the jeera, rai and chopped onion. Cook together until the onion is golden brown.
2. Add the tomato purée, turmeric powder, chilli powder, garam masala, salt, garlic powder, mixed vegetables and potatoes. Stir continuously and cook for a further 5 minutes.
3. Add the water to the vegetables, and bring to the boil. Reduce the heat and simmer gently for about 20 minutes.
4. Serve hot.

MADRAS POTATO AND PEA CURRY

Serves 4.

Preparation and cooking time: 30 mins.

This is one of the many vegetable dishes served with another main dish and rice.

340g (12oz) potatoes
60ml (2fl oz) cooking oil
$^1/_2$ tsp whole jeera (cumin seeds)
$^1/_2$ tsp whole rai (black mustard seeds)
2 large onions, finely chopped
170g (6oz) frozen peas
$^1/_2$ tsp chilli powder
$^1/_2$ tsp turmeric powder
1 tsp madras curry powder
1 tsp salt
2 tsp tomato purée
300ml (10fl oz) water
Small amount green dhanyia (coriander), chopped

Method
1. Peel the potatoes and cut them into about 2.5cm (1 inch) cubes.
2. Heat the oil to a high temperature in a large pan. Add jeera, rai and onions. Stir continuously and cook until the onions are golden brown. Add potatoes, peas, chilli powder, turmeric powder, madras curry powder, salt and tomato purée. Stir continuously for 2 minutes. Add the water and bring to the boil. Lower the heat and simmer gently for about 20 minutes.
3. Transfer the curry to a serving dish and garnish with fresh green dhanyia.

GUJARATI POTATO CURRY

Serves 4.

Preparation and cooking time: 35 mins.

This is a very popular curry in a part of India which is well known for its vegetable dishes. It is usually served with some other curry (such as dhal or meat) and rice.

450g (1lb) potatoes
30ml (1fl oz) cooking oil
$^1/_2$ tsp whole jeera (cumin seeds)
$^1/_2$ tsp whole rai (black mustard seeds)
$^1/_4$ tsp hing (asafoetida)
$^1/_2$ tsp turmeric powder
$^1/_2$ tsp jeera powder (cumin powder)
$^1/_2$ tsp dhanyia powder (coriander powder)
1 tsp salt
1 tsp red chilli powder
55g (2oz) tinned tomatoes or 2 tsp tomato purée
450ml (15fl oz) water
Small amount green dhanyia (coriander), chopped

Method

1. Peel the potatoes and cut into about 2.5cm (1 inch) cubes.
2. Heat the oil to a high temperature in a large pan and add the jeera, rai and asafoetida. Leave to cook for a few seconds. Add the potatoes, turmeric powder, jeera powder, dhanyia powder, salt, chilli powder, and tomatoes (or purée). Stir continuously and cook for about 5 minutes.
3. Add the water and bring it to the boil. Lower the heat and simmer gently for about 20 minutes.
4. Place the curry in a serving dish and garnish with fresh dhanyia.

PUNJABI POTATO CURRY

Serves 4.

Preparation and cooking time: 35 mins.

This is a popular curry in northern parts of India. It is usually served with parothas or puris (deep fried chapattis – see recipe on page 202).

450g (1lb) potatoes
25g (1oz) butter
1 large onion, finely chopped
2 green chillies, finely chopped
1 tsp turmeric powder
1 tsp ginger powder
$^1/_2$ tsp dhanyia powder (coriander powder)
1 tsp salt
$^1/_2$ tsp chilli powder
4 tsp tomato purée
240ml (8fl oz) water
Small amount green dhanyia (coriander), chopped

Method

1. Peel the potatoes.
2. Boil the potatoes, and cut them into 2.5cm (1 inch) cubes.
3. Melt the butter in a large pan and add the onion and chillies. Stir and cook the onion and chillies until the onion is light brown. Now add the turmeric powder, ginger powder, dhanyia powder, salt, chilli powder, and tomato purée. Stir continuously and cook for about 2 minutes. Add half of the water, stir, and add the potatoes. Mix well and let it cook for about 3 minutes.
4. Add the remaining water and bring it to the boil. Lower the heat and simmer gently for about 5 minutes. .
5. Place the curry in a serving dish and garnish with fresh dhanyia.

BOMBAY POTATO CURRY

Serves 4.

Preparation and cooking time: 35 mins.

This is a common curry in most Indian restaurants. It is very simple to cook and usually served with some other curry (such as dhal or meat) and rice.

450g (1lb) potatoes
30ml (1fl oz) cooking oil
1 tsp whole jeera (cumin seeds)
$^1/_2$ tsp whole rai (black mustard seeds)
$^1/_2$ tsp turmeric powder
1 tsp salt
$^1/_2$ tsp chilli powder
110g (4oz) fresh tomatoes, finely chopped
150ml (5fl oz) water
Small amount green dhanyia (coriander), chopped

Method
1. Peel the potatoes and cut into 2.5cm (1 inch) cubes.
2. Heat the oil to a high temperature in a large pan and add the jeera, and rai. Leave to cook for a few seconds. Add the potatoes, turmeric powder, salt, chilli powder and tomatoes. Stir continuously and cook for about 5 minutes.
3. Add the water and bring to the boil. Lower the heat and simmer gently for about 20 minutes.
4. Place the curry in a serving dish and garnish with fresh dhanyia.

GUJARATI GREEN BEAN CURRY

Serves 4.

Preparation and cooking time: 15 mins.

A large proportion of the residents of the Gujarat state of India are vegetarians and they have therefore improvised on many of the standard dhal and vegetable dishes. Green beans are one of their specialties.

60ml (2fl oz) cooking oil
$^1/_2$ tsp whole rai (black mustard seeds)
$^1/_2$ tsp whole jeera (cumin seeds)
$^1/_4$ tsp hing (asafoetida)
55g (2oz) fresh tomatoes, finely chopped
$^1/_2$ tsp salt
$^1/_2$ tsp turmeric powder
$^1/_2$ tsp jeera powder (cumin)
$^1/_2$ tsp dhanyia powder (coriander)
$^1/_2$ tsp chilli powder
340g (12oz) frozen green beans, thawed
120ml (4fl oz) water

Method
1. Heat the oil to a high temperature in a large pan. Add the rai, jeera and asafoetida and let it cook for a few seconds. Add the tomatoes, salt, turmeric powder, jeera powder, dhanyia powder and chilli powder. Let this spice mixture cook for about 2 minutes.
2. Add the beans, mix well and then add the water. Bring the water to the boil, lower the heat and let the beans simmer for about 8 minutes, stirring every 2 to 3 minutes.
3. Transfer the contents to a serving dish and serve hot.

FRESH MIXED VEGETABLE CURRY

Serves 4.

Preparation and cooking time: 45 mins.

This is a very hot vegetable curry usually served with rice. For this recipe you need a liquidizer.

340g (12oz) potatoes
1 large aubergine approx 225g (8oz)
110g (4oz) plum peeled tomatoes
25g (1oz) fresh garlic, peeled
55g (2oz) fresh ginger, peeled
60ml (2fl oz) cooking oil
$^1/_2$ tsp whole jeera (cumin seeds)
$^1/_2$ tsp whole rai (black mustard seeds)
$^1/_2$ tsp turmeric powder
1 tsp garam masala
$1^1/_2$ tsp salt
$^3/_4$ tsp chilli powder
8 green chillies
170g (6oz) frozen peas, thawed
600ml (20fl oz) water
Small portion of fresh green dhanyia (coriander)

Method

1. Peel the potatoes and cut them into 2.5cm (1 inch) cubes.
2. Remove the stalk of the aubergine and cut into 2.5cm (1 inch) cubes.
3. Place the tomatoes, garlic, and ginger into a liquidizer and blend into a thickish paste.
4. Heat the oil to a high temperature in a pan. Add the jeera and rai and leave it cooking for a few seconds. Add the thick paste, turmeric powder, garam masala, salt, chilli powder, potatoes, aubergine, green chillies and peas. Stir continuously and cook for about 5 minutes.
5. Add the water, bring it to the boil and simmer gently for about 30 minutes.
6. Place the curry in a serving dish and garnish with fresh dhanyia.

AUBERGINE AND POTATO CURRY (DRY)

Serves 4.

Preparation and cooking time: 35 mins.

This is a mild vegetable curry, especially – good when served with a meat dish. It is also excellent for vegetarians. It is usually served with rice or chapattis. Parsley or fresh coriander can be used for garnishing.

450g (1lb) potatoes
1 large aubergine approx 225g (8oz)
2 large onions
60ml (2fl oz) cooking oil
$^1/_2$ tsp whole jeera (cumin seeds)
$^1/_2$ tsp whole rai (black mustard seeds)
2 tsp tomato purée
1 tsp salt
$^1/_2$ tsp turmeric powder
$^1/_2$ tsp chilli powder
1 tsp tandoori masala
1 tsp garam masala
90ml (3fl oz) water
Fresh parsley or green fresh dhanyia (coriander), finely chopped

Method

1. Peel the potatoes and cut them into large chips.
2. Remove the stalk and cut the aubergine into large chip type pieces also.
3. Chop the onions into small pieces.
4. Heat the oil to a high temperature in a large pan. Add the jeera and rai to the oil and cook until they are golden brown. This will only take a few seconds.
5. Add the chopped onions. Cook together until the onions are golden brown. Add the tomato purée, salt, turmeric powder, chilli powder, tandoori masala, garam masala, potatoes and aubergine pieces. Stir and cook for another few minutes. Reduce the heat.
6. Add the water; bring to the boil, cover the pan and simmer gently for about 30 to 35 minutes, stirring every 5 to 7 minutes. Switch off the heat and place the cooked curry in a serving dish.
7. Garnish with parsley or fresh coriander.

AUBERGINE AND PEA CURRY

Serves 4.

Preparation and cooking time: 25 mins.

This is a mild curry usually served with chapattis, parothas or another meat dish.

450g (1lb) aubergines
600ml (20fl oz) water for soaking
60ml (2fl oz) cooking oil
$^1/_2$ tsp whole rai (black mustard seeds)
$^1/_2$ tsp whole jeera (cumin seeds)
2 tsp tomato purée
1 tsp turmeric powder
1 tsp salt
1 tsp chilli powder
1 tsp garam masala
1 tsp garlic powder
120ml (4fl oz) water
225g (8oz) frozen peas
2 tsp lemon juice
Small amount green dhanyia (coriander), chopped

Method

1. Remove the stalks from the aubergines and slice them lengthways, like large chips. Soak the aubergines in the 600ml (20fl oz) of water for about 5 minutes.

2. Heat the oil to a high temperature in a heavy-based saucepan. Add the whole rai and whole jeera and let it cook for a few seconds.

3. Remove the aubergines from the water and add them to the pot. Now add the tomato purée, turmeric powder, salt, chilli powder, garam masala and garlic powder. Mix well and cook for about 2 to 3 minutes.

4. Add the 120ml (4fl oz) of water, cover the pan, reduce the heat and let the aubergines simmer for about 10 minutes, stirring every 4 to 5 minutes.

5. Add the peas and the lemon juice. Simmer for a further 7 minutes, stirring every 3 to 4 minutes.

6. Transfer the contents to a serving dish and serve while hot.

AUBERGINE AND SPINACH BHARTHA
(Mashed aubergine and spinach)

Serves 4.

Preparation and cooking time: 1 hr 10 mins.

Bharthas are usually served with chapattis or as a side dish. This is a hot vegetable dish.

450g (1lb) aubergines
450g (1lb) fresh spinach
60ml (2fl oz) cooking oil
1 large onion, finely chopped
110g (4oz) plum peeled tomatoes, finely chopped
1 tsp salt
1 tsp turmeric powder
1 tsp chilli powder
1 tsp dhanyia powder (coriander)
1 tsp jeera powder (cumin)
1 tsp garlic powder

Method

1. Prick the aubergines with a fork and then roast them under the grill for about 30 minutes, turning every 7 to 8 minutes. When the aubergines have been well roasted, remove the stalks, peel the aubergines and cut into very small pieces or mash them.
2. Wash the spinach, and chop finely.
3. Heat the oil to a high temperature in a large pan. Add the onion and cook, stirring continuously, until the onion is golden brown. Add the mashed aubergine, spinach, tomatoes, salt, turmeric powder, chilli powder, dhanyia powder, jeera powder, and garlic powder. Stir and mix well. Lower the heat, cover the pan and let it simmer for about 25 minutes, stirring every 5 to 7 minutes.
4. Transfer the contents to a serving dish and serve while hot.

CAULIFLOWER AND POTATO CURRY (DRY)

Serves 4.

Preparation and cooking time: 35 mins.

This is a mild vegetable curry, especially good when served with a meat and dhal dish. It is also very popular with vegetarians. It is usually served with rice, chapattis or bread.

340g (12oz) potatoes
340g (12oz) cauliflower (1 medium cauliflower)
60ml (2fl oz) cooking oil
$^1/_2$ tsp whole jeera (cumin seeds)
$^1/_2$ tsp whole rai (black mustard seeds)
1 tsp turmeric powder
1 tsp garam masala
2 tsp tomato purée
1 tsp salt
$^1/_2$ tsp chilli powder
120ml (4fl oz) water
Small amount green dhanyia (coriander), chopped

Method
1. Peel the potatoes and cut them into 2.5cm (1 inch) cubes.
2. Cut the cauliflower into small florets.
3. Heat the oil to a high temperature in a pan. Add the jeera and rai and leave to cook for a few seconds. Add potatoes, cauliflower, turmeric powder, garam masala, tomato purée, salt and chilli powder. Stir continuously and cook for about 3 minutes.
4. Add the water, bring it to the boil and simmer gently for about 15 minutes.
5. Place the curry in a serving dish and garnish with fresh dhanyia.

FRESH SPINACH CURRY

Serves 4.

Preparation and cooking time: 25 mins.

If you like spinach, then you must try this dish. It can be served instead of boiled spinach or, like other vegetable curries, with chapattis or a side dish.

60ml (2fl oz) cooking oil
1 small onion, finely chopped
450g (1lb) fresh spinach, finely chopped
$^1/_2$ tsp turmeric powder
$^1/_2$ tsp chilli powder
$^1/_2$ tsp salt
$^1/_2$ tsp garam masala
$^1/_2$ tsp garlic powder
1 tsp tomato purée
1 tomato, cut into small pieces

Method
1. Heat the oil to a high temperature in a large pan. Add the onion and cook until the onion is golden brown. Add the spinach, turmeric powder, chilli powder, salt, garam masala, garlic powder and tomato purée. Mix well, cover the pan, lower the heat, and let it simmer for about 15 minutes, stirring every 4 to 5 minutes.
2. Transfer the spinach to a serving dish and garnish with the tomato.

WHITE CABBAGE CURRY

Serves 4.

Preparation and cooking time: 40 mins.

This is a hot vegetable curry usually served with a rice dish, or chapattis. It also makes an excellent filling for toasted sandwiches. For this recipe you need a liquidizer.

25g (1oz) fresh garlic, peeled
55g (2oz) fresh ginger, peeled
6 whole green chillies
60ml (2fl oz) cooking oil
$^{1}/_{2}$ tsp whole jeera (cumin seeds)
$^{1}/_{2}$ tsp whole rai (black mustard seeds)
4 whole cloves
4 whole black peppercorns
$^{1}/_{4}$ tsp hing (asafoetida)
670g (1$^{1}/_{2}$lb) white cabbage, shredded
2 tsp tomato purée
$^{1}/_{2}$ tsp turmeric powder
$^{1}/_{2}$ tsp chilli powder
1 tsp garam masala
1 tsp salt
4 tsp soy sauce
180ml (6fl oz) water

Method

1. Place the garlic, ginger, and green chillies in a liquidizer, and chop finely.
2. Heat the oil to a high temperature in a wok or large pan, and add the jeera, rai, whole cloves, whole peppercorns, and asafoetida. Cook for a few seconds.
3. Add the cabbage, tomato purée, turmeric powder, chilli powder, garam masala, salt and soy sauce. Cook for a further few seconds.
4. Add the contents of the liquidizer and water to the cabbage.
5. Stir well and bring the mixture to the boil. Cover the pan, reduce the heat and simmer gently for about 20 minutes, stirring every 5 to 7 minutes.
6. Transfer the contents to a serving dish and serve hot.
7. The cloves are discarded and left at the side of the plate while eating.

TINDORA CURRY

Serves 4.

Preparation and cooking time: 20 mins.

This is a very unusual curry, and tastes like courgettes or cucumber. If you are prepared to try something new, then this may be to your taste. It is usually served with rice or chapattis. For this recipe you need a liquidizer.

85g (3oz) fresh garlic, peeled
85g (3oz) fresh ginger, peeled
4 whole green chillies
450g (1lb) fresh tindora (see introduction, page 17)
60ml (2fl oz) cooking oil
$^1/_2$ tsp whole jeera (cumin seeds)
$^1/_2$ tsp whole rai (black mustard seeds)
$^1/_4$ tsp hing (asafoetida)
2 tsp tomato purée
1 tsp salt
$^1/_2$ tsp turmeric powder
1 tsp chilli powder
1 tsp garam masala
4 tsp soy sauce
300ml (10fl oz) water
1 fresh tomato, cut into small pieces for garnishing

Method

1. Place the garlic, ginger, and green chillies into a liquidizer and chop finely.
2. Cut each fresh tindora into four pieces.
3. Heat the oil to a high temperature in a large pan, and add the jeera, rai and asafoetida. Fry for a few seconds.
4. Add the cut tindora, contents of the liquidizer, tomato purée, salt, turmeric powder, chilli powder, garam masala and soy sauce. Stir and cook for about 2 minutes. Add the water, and bring to the boil. Reduce the heat, cover the pan and simmer gently for about 7 minutes.
5. Transfer the contents to a serving dish and garnish with the tomato.

VALLOUR VEGETABLE CURRY

Serves 4.

Preparation and cooking time: 35 mins.

This is an unusual vegetable curry and tastes very similar to courgettes. It is usually served with chapattis or with another dhal curry and rice.

2 medium size potatoes
340g (12oz) fresh vallour (see introduction, page 17)
60ml (2fl oz) cooking oil
1 tsp whole rai (black mustard seeds)
1 tsp whole jeera (cumin seeds)
$^1/_4$ tsp hing (asafoetida)
2 tsp tomato purée
$^1/_2$ tsp chilli powder
1 tsp salt
$1^1/_2$ tsp garam masala
$^1/_2$ tsp turmeric powder
1 tsp garlic powder
1 tsp tandoori masala
300ml (10fl oz) water
1 fresh tomato, cut into small pieces for garnishing

Method

1. Peel the potatoes and cut into about 2.5cm (1 inch) cubes.
2. Top and tail the vallour and cut them lengthways into about 2.5cm (1 inch) long pieces.
3. Heat the oil in a wok or pan and add the rai, jeera and asafoetida. Cook for a few seconds. Add the potatoes, vallour, tomato purée, chilli powder, salt, garam masala, turmeric powder, garlic powder and tandoori masala. Stir continuously and cook for a further 5 minutes.
4. Add the water; bring it to the boil, reduce the heat and simmer gently for a further 20 minutes.
5. Transfer the contents to a serving dish and garnish with the tomato. Serve while hot.

GREEN PEPPER WITH NEW POTATO CURRY

Serves 4.

Preparation and cooking time: 35 mins.

This is a very mild vegetable curry and can be served with chapattis, or dhal curries and rice. It tastes especially good with new potatoes, but ordinary potatoes can be used.

60ml (2fl oz) cooking oil
$^1/_2$ tsp whole jeera (cumin seeds)
1 onion, finely chopped
225g (8oz) new potatoes, peeled and cut into very thin discs, like crisps
2 large green peppers, sliced in rings like crisps
1 tsp salt
$^1/_2$ tsp turmeric powder
$^1/_2$ tsp garam masala
90ml (3fl oz) water
1 tsp tomato purée
$^1/_2$ tsp chilli powder

Method
1. Heat the oil to a high temperature in a wok or a deep pan. Add the jeera, cook for a few seconds and add the onion. Cook until golden brown.
2. Add the potatoes, peppers, salt, turmeric powder, garam masala, water, tomato purée, and the chilli powder. Mix well.
3. Bring the water to the boil, lower the heat and cover the pan. Simmer gently for about 20 minutes, stirring every 5 to 7 minutes.
4. Transfer the contents to serving dish and serve while hot.

GUAER CURRY

Serves 4.

Preparation and cooking time: 45 mins.

It is difficult to describe the flavour of guaer. The closest approximation is that it tastes similar to green beans.

225g (8oz) guaer (see introduction, page 17)
60ml (2fl oz) cooking oil
$^1/_2$ tsp whole rai (black mustard seeds)
$^1/_2$ tsp whole jeera (cumin seeds)
$^1/_4$ tsp hing (asafoetida)
2 tsp tomato purée
1 tsp salt
1 tsp turmeric powder
1 tsp jeera powder (cumin)
1 tsp dhanyia powder (coriander)
1 tsp chilli powder
450ml (15fl oz) water

Method
1. Top and tail the guaer and then cut into about 2cm (1 inch) lengths.
2. Heat the oil to a high temperature in a large pan. Add the rai, jeera and asafoetida and let it cook for a few seconds. Add the tomato purée, salt, turmeric powder, jeera powder, dhanyia powder and chilli powder. Let this spice mixture cook for about 2 minutes.
3. Add the guaer, mix well and then add the water. Lower the heat and let the guaer simmer for about 30 minutes, stirring every 5 to 6 minutes.
4. Transfer the contents to a serving dish and serve hot.

KADU AND TOMATO CURRY

Serves 4.

Preparation and cooking time: 25 mins.

Kadu tastes somewhat similar to marrow. This is a very mild curry usually served with chapattis.

225g (8oz) kadu (see introduction, page 17)
60ml (2fl oz) cooking oil
$^1/_2$ tsp whole rai (black mustard seeds)
$^1/_2$ tsp whole jeera (cumin seeds)
110g (4oz) fresh tomatoes, finely chopped
$^1/_2$ tsp salt
$^1/_2$ tsp turmeric powder
$^1/_2$ tsp garam masala
$^1/_2$ tsp chilli powder

Method
1. Peel the kadu and cut into about 2cm (1 inch) cubes.
2. Heat the oil to a high temperature in a large pan. Add the rai and jeera and let it cook for a few seconds. Add the tomatoes, salt, turmeric powder, garam masala and chilli powder. Let this spice mixture cook for about 1 minute.
3. Add the kadu. Lower the heat and let the kadu simmer for about 30 minutes, stirring every 5 to 7 minutes.
4. Transfer the contents to a serving dish. Serve hot.

6

RAITAS, CHUTNEYS AND PICKLES

Raitas, made from fresh natural yoghurt, are very common in Indian homes. Most Indians make fresh yoghurt themselves, and fresh yoghurt made at home tastes different. Yoghurt is usually made in the evenings and left to 'set' overnight. Raita can then be made in the morning.

PLAIN FRESH NATURAL YOGHURT

Makes 600ml (20fl oz).

Preparation and cooking time: 8 hrs 30 mins.

600ml (20fl oz) milk
30ml (1fl oz) natural yoghurt

Method
1. Bring the milk to the boil in a large pan. Leave it to cool for about 10 minutes, so that the milk is warm, before going to the next step.
2. Transfer the milk into a bowl with a cover. Add the yoghurt and mix well. Cover the bowl and leave the mixture in a warm place, such as the airing cupboard, for about 8 hours.
3. The setting process may take longer than 8 hours if the temperature is not warm enough.

POTATO AND ONION RAITA

Serves 4.

Preparation and cooking time: 30 mins.

All raitas are served as side dishes and are especially good in the summer.

340g (12oz) boiled potatoes
1 large onion, finely chopped
1 green chilli, finely chopped
450ml (15fl oz) plain, fresh natural yoghurt
90ml (3fl oz) cold, fresh milk
$^1/_2$ tsp salt
$^1/_2$ tsp chilli powder
$^1/_2$ tsp black pepper

Method
1. Cut the boiled potatoes into small pieces.
2. Place the potatoes, onion and green chilli into a serving dish. Add the yoghurt and milk, and mix well.
3. Place the raita in a fridge.
4. When you are ready to serve, remove the raita from the fridge and add the salt, chilli powder and black pepper. Mix well and serve.

ONION AND CUCUMBER RAITA

Serves 4.

Preparation and cooking time: 15 mins.

450ml (15fl oz) plain fresh natural yoghurt
90ml (3fl oz) cold milk
110g (4oz) cucumber, peeled and sliced
1 large onion, chopped into small pieces
$^1/_2$ tsp whole jeera (cumin seeds)
$^1/_2$ tsp salt
$^1/_2$ tsp chilli powder
$^1/_2$ tsp black ground pepper

Method
1. Combine the yoghurt and milk in a serving dish and mix well.
2. Add the sliced cucumber, onion and whole jeera. Mix well.
3. Place the raita in a fridge.
4. When ready to serve, mix salt, chilli powder and black ground pepper into the raita.

GARLIC CHUTNEY

Makes about 450g (1lb) of chutney.

Preparation and cooking time: 40 mins.

Garlic chutneys are not served at meals but are used in cooking many curry dishes. Instead of blending garlic and ginger in a liquidizer, a spoonful of garlic chutney can be used instead. This saves having to peel garlic and ginger every time. You need a liquidizer to prepare this chutney.

60ml (2fl oz) water
110g (4oz) green chillies
170g (6oz) fresh ginger, peeled
110g (4oz) fresh garlic, peeled
1^1/$_2$ tsp salt
60ml (2fl oz) lemon juice

Method
1.   Place all the ingredients in a liquidizer and blend together.
2.   Transfer the contents into a jar, and store in a fridge. This chutney can be kept for up to 3 weeks.

FRESH MINT CHUTNEY

Serves 4.

Preparation and cooking time: 15 mins.

This is a mild chutney, often served with main meals. Sugar can be added to give it a slightly sweeter taste. Either anardana or lemon can be used. A liquidizer or blender is needed to prepare this chutney.

55g (2oz) fresh mint leaves
1 small onion, finely chopped
$^1/_2$ tsp salt
$^1/_2$ tsp whole jeera (cumin seeds)
$^1/_2$ tsp sugar (optional)
$^1/_2$ tsp anardana (pomegranate seeds) or $^1/_2$ tsp lemon juice
10g ($^1/_2$oz) green chillies
30ml (1fl oz) water

Method
1. Place all the ingredients in a liquidizer and blend them into a smooth paste.
2. Transfer the contents to a serving dish.
3. Like all chutneys this can be stored in a cool place and served again. This chutney must be used in 3 to 4 days.

FRESH MINT AND APPLE CHUTNEY

Serves 4.

Preparation and cooking time: 15 mins.

Chutneys are usually served with all main meals as a small side dish, like pickles. This is a hot chutney and is very good with most rice dishes. Sugar can be added to give it a slightly sweeter taste. A liquidizer or blender is needed to prepare this chutney.

55g (2oz) mint leaves
110g (4oz) cooking apples, finely chopped
55g (2oz) onions, finely chopped
55g (2oz) green chillies
$^3/_4$ tsp salt
30ml (1fl oz) water
$^1/_2$ tsp turmeric powder
$^1/_2$ tsp sugar (optional)

Method
1. Place all the ingredients in a liquidizer and blend them into a smooth paste.
2. Transfer the contents into a small serving dish and place in the fridge for a couple of hours.
3. The chutney is ready to be served. Unused chutney can be left in the fridge, and served again. This chutney must be used within 7 days.

GREEN CHILLI PICKLE (FRIED)

Serves 4.

Preparation and cooking time: 20 mins.

Sugar can be added to give the pickle a slightly sweeter taste.

55g (2oz) green chillies
30ml (1fl oz) cooking oil
$^1/_4$ tsp whole jeera (cumin seeds)
$^1/_4$ tsp whole rai (black mustard seeds)
$^1/_4$ tsp hing (asafoetida)
$^1/_2$ tsp salt
$^1/_2$ tsp turmeric powder
15ml ($^1/_2$fl oz) lemon juice
$^1/_2$ tsp sugar (optional)
30ml (1fl oz) water

Method
1. Remove the stems and slice the chillies into halves lengthways. (Remember to wash hands thoroughly after handling the chillies otherwise the chillies leave a burning sensation on them.)
2. Place the cooking oil in a frying pan. Heat the oil to a high temperature; add the jeera, rai, and asafoetida. Leave to cook for a few seconds until they are slightly brown. Add the chillies, salt, turmeric powder, lemon juice, sugar (if used) and water. Bring to the boil. Reduce the heat and simmer for about 5 minutes.
3. Place the cooked chillies in a serving dish.

FRESH GREEN CHILLI PICKLE

Serves 4.

Preparation and cooking time: 10 mins.

55g (2oz) green chillies
1^1/$_2$ tsp salt
1^1/$_2$ tsp rai dhal (split black mustard)
^{1}/$_2$ tsp turmeric powder
1 tsp cooking oil
60ml (2fl oz) lemon juice
^{1}/$_4$ tsp hing (asafoetida)

Method
1. Remove the stems and slice the chillies into halves lengthways. (Remember to wash hands thoroughly after handling the chillies otherwise they leave a burning sensation on them.)
2. Mix well all the ingredients together with the cut chillies in a large bowl, and then transfer the contents to an airtight tin.
3. This pickle can be stored for up to 2 weeks if kept in an airtight tin and placed in the fridge. Use as and when needed.

LEMON AND GREEN CHILLI PICKLE

Serves 4.

Preparation and cooking time: 4 days

This is a pickle in which lemon and fresh green chillies are allowed to marinate in their own juices for about 3–4 days. It is not spicy, but very hot.

55g (2oz) green chillies
4 tsp salt for green chillies
2 fresh lemons
1 tsp salt for lemons

Method
1. Remove the stems and cut open one side of the chillies along the length, so that the chillies still remain whole. (Remember to wash hands thoroughly after handling the chillies otherwise they leave a burning sensation on them.)
2. With a teaspoon fill the chillies with salt. The four teaspoonfuls of salt should be enough to fill all the chillies.
3. Slice the lemons into quarters. but do not cut them right through. Leave about 0.5cm ($^1/_4$ inch) at the bottom where the lemon is not cut. Ensure that the lemon still remains in one piece.
4. Now share the teaspoonful of salt between the two lemons.
5. Transfer both the lemons and the chillies to an airtight tin and leave it in a cool place (not the fridge) for about 4 days. The salt will draw out the juices from the lemons and chillies and these will marinate in their own juices.
6. This pickle can be stored for up to 2 weeks if kept in an airtight tin and placed in the fridge. Use as and when needed.

CARROT, WHITE CABBAGE AND GREEN CHILLI PICKLE

Serves 4.

Preparation and cooking time: 30 mins.

Of the many Indian pickles served with main meals, this is one of the few prepared fresh, and served hot. Sugar can be added to give the pickle a slightly sweeter taste.

30ml (1fl oz) cooking oil
¼ tsp whole jeera (cumin seeds)
¼ tsp whole rai (black mustard seeds)
¼ tsp hing (asafoetida)
4 small green chillies cut into halves lengthways
55g (2oz) white cabbage, shredded
4 small carrots, cut into long, thin strips
1 tsp sugar (optional)
$^1/_2$ tsp salt
$^1/_2$ tsp turmeric powder
$^1/_2$ tsp tomato purée
90ml (3fl oz) water
30ml (1fl oz) lemon juice

Method

1. Heat the oil to a high temperature in a frying pan, and add the jeera, rai and asafoetida. Cook for a few seconds.
2. Add the chillies, cabbage, carrots, sugar (if used), salt, turmeric powder and tomato purée and cook for a further 2 minutes, stirring continuously. Add the water, and bring the mixture to the boil. Reduce the heat, and simmer gently until the water has evaporated. This will take about 15 minutes. Add the lemon juice and cook for a further 1 minute, stirring all the time.
3. Transfer the contents to a serving dish.

CARROT PICKLE

Serves 4.

Preparation and cooking time: 15 mins.

225g (8oz) carrots
1 tsp salt
$^1/_2$ tsp turmeric powder
30ml (1fl oz) cooking oil
30ml (1fl oz) lemon juice
2 tsp rai dhal (split mustard)
$^1/_4$ tsp hing (asafoetida)

Method
1. Peel the carrots; wash them and cut them into 2.5cm (1 inch) long strips about 0.5cm ($^1/_4$ inch) thick.
2. Add all the above spices to the carrots, mix well, and transfer the contents to an airtight tin.
3. This pickle can be stored for up to 2 weeks if kept in an airtight tin and placed in the fridge. Use as and when needed.

APPLE PICKLE

Serves 4.

Preparation and cooking time: 15 mins.

225g (8oz) cooking apples
15ml ($^1/_2$fl oz) cooking oil
1 tsp salt
$^1/_4$ tsp garam masala
$^1/_4$ tsp ground jeera (cumin seeds)
$^1/_2$ tsp rai dhal (split mustard)
$^1/_4$ tsp hing (asafoetida)
15ml ($^1/_2$fl oz) lemon juice

Method
1. Peel the apples and cut them into about 1cm ($^1/_2$ inch) cubes.
2. Heat the oil in a pan. Add the salt, garam masala, ground jeera, rai dhal and asafoetida. Cook for a few seconds.
3. Switch off the heat, add the apples and lemon juice and mix well.
4. Transfer the contents to an airtight tin.
5. This pickle can be stored for up to 1 week if kept in an airtight tin and placed in the fridge. Use as and when needed.

7

MISCELLANEOUS

CHAPATTIS

Makes about 15 chapattis.

Preparation and cooking time: 30 mins.

Chapattis are a good substitute for bread and can be served with almost any curry. For this recipe you need a large flat frying pan or tava.

450g (1lb) white chapatti flour (sieved)
30ml (1fl oz) cooking oil
210ml (7fl oz) water
55g (2oz) chapatti flour, for rolling
55g (2oz) butter

Method
1. Place the sieved flour in a bowl and add the cooking oil. Mix together for a few seconds.
2. Add water gradually, and continue to mix until a stiff or medium soft dough is formed, which can be kneaded.
3. Divide the mixture into about 15 balls, sprinkle flour on the rolling area and roll each ball into a disc of about 17.5cm (7 inches) diameter.
4. Heat a tava or large flat pan to a high temperature. Place the chapatti on it, leave it for a few seconds and turn it over. After a few seconds turn and cook the first side again, until it turns light brown in colour. Repeat for the other side. The cooking process takes approximately 15 seconds for each side. Remove the chapatti from the pan and place it on a plate. Butter one side of each chapatti, and stack one on top of another. Serve them hot.

BHATURAS

Serves 4.

Preparation and cooking time: 4 hrs 40 mins.

Bhaturas can be served with almost any curry dish, but are usually served with chana, and raita. They taste like very soft bread, and are served instead of chapattis or puris (deep fried chapattis). For this recipe you need a deep frying pan or wok.

450g (1lb) plain flour, sieved for dough
1 tsp baking powder, sieved
300ml (10fl oz) plain yoghurt
55g (2oz) plain flour, for rolling
600ml (20fl oz) cooking oil, for deep frying

Method
1. Mix the flour, baking powder and yoghurt in a large mixing bowl, and make a medium soft dough. Leave the dough covered for 4 hours.
2. Divide the dough into about 12 equal parts.
3. Shape each part into a ball, flour the surface of the balls well with dry flour. Roll the balls flat into about 0.5cm ($^1/_4$ inch) thick, 14cm (5 to 6 inches) diameter discs.
4. Heat the oil to a high temperature in a wok or deep frying pan, and then reduce the heat. Deep fry the rolled bhatura, which will float, one at a time, for about $^1/_2$ minute on each side. Drain the oil from the bhatura and place in a serving dish. Repeat this with all the bhaturas.
5. Serve hot.

FRIED RICE

Serves 4.

Preparation and cooking time: 1 hr 30 mins.

Fried rice can feature as a snack or at high tea, without curry or dhals.
Left over plain boiled rice can also be fried in the manner described
below. For this recipe you need a large wok or deep frying pan.

170g (6oz) plain basmati rice
1500ml (50fl oz) water
60ml (2fl oz) cooking oil
$^1/_2$ tsp whole rai (black mustard seeds)
$^1/_2$ tsp whole jeera (cumin seeds)
$^1/_4$ tsp hing (asafoetida)
1 small onion, finely chopped
1 small potato, chopped into very small pieces
$^1/_2$ tsp turmeric powder
1 tsp salt
$^1/_2$ tsp chilli powder
1 large tomato, cut into rings, for garnishing

Method

1. Wash the rice and leave to soak in the 1500ml (50fl oz) of water for about 1 hour.
2. Bring the water containing the rice to the boil, and then simmer gently for a further 15 minutes.
3. Transfer the contents to a colander to drain the rice.
4. Heat the oil in a big wok or a deep frying pan. Add the rai, jeera and asafoetida, and cook them for a few seconds. Add the onion and cook until it is golden brown. Add the potato and cook over a low heat for about 10 minutes. Make sure that the potato is well cooked.
5. Add the rice, turmeric powder, salt and chilli powder and stir well. Cook the whole mixture together for a further 3 minutes stirring continuously.
6. Transfer the contents to a serving dish. Garnish with the fresh tomato and serve hot.

CHICKEN BIRYANI

Serves 4.

Preparation and cooking time: 1 hr 20 mins.

This is a mild rice dish, quick to make and popular with busy housewives. It is usually served with fresh salad. For this recipe you need a wok, or deep frying pan, and a liquidizer.

25g (1oz) fresh garlic, peeled
55g (2oz) fresh ginger, peeled
900ml (30fl oz) chicken stock
170g (6oz) basmati rice
3 large chicken pieces
120ml (4fl oz) cooking oil
3 whole cloves
4 whole black peppercorns
$^1/_2$ tsp whole jeera (cumin seeds)
$^1/_2$ tsp whole rai (black mustard seeds)
$^1/_4$ tsp hing (asafoetida)
1 onion, finely chopped
1 tsp tomato purée
85g (3oz) frozen peas
1 small carrot, sliced thinly
$^1/_2$ tsp turmeric powder
1 tsp salt
$^1/_2$ tsp chilli powder

Method

1. Place the garlic and ginger in a liquidizer and chop finely. Add the contents of the liquidizer to the 900ml (30fl oz) of chicken stock and mix well.

2. Wash the rice like all dhals (see page 16).

3. Remove the skin and bones from the chicken and cut the chicken into small pieces, about 7.5cm (3 inches) long.

4. Heat 60ml (2fl oz) of cooking oil to a high temperature in a wok or deep frying pan; add the chicken pieces and cook over a low heat until the chicken pieces are golden brown.

5. In another separate pan heat the remaining 60ml (2fl oz) of oil to a high temperature. Add the cloves, peppercorns, jeera, rai, and asafoetida and cook for a few seconds. Add the chopped onion, and cook until the onion is golden brown. Add the rice, cooked chicken, tomato purée, peas, carrot, turmeric powder, salt and chilli powder. Cook for a further 2 minutes, stirring continuously.

6. Add the stock mixture to the rice. Bring it to the boil and reduce the heat. Cover the pan and simmer gently for about 15 minutes. The rice should now look pretty dry.

7. Transfer the contents to a serving dish and serve while hot.

8. The cloves and peppercorns are discarded while eating and left on the plate.

PEA PILAW RICE

Serves 4.

Preparation and cooking time: 1 hr 30 mins.

This is one of the many rice dishes usually served with any curry or dhal.

170g (6oz) basmati rice
390ml (13fl oz) water
60ml (2fl oz) cooking oil
$^1/_2$ tsp whole jeera (cumin seeds)
$^1/_2$ tsp whole rai (black mustard seeds)
$^1/_2$ tsp salt
$^1/_2$ tsp turmeric powder
$^1/_2$ tsp chilli powder
1 tsp tomato purée
55g (3oz) frozen peas

Method
1. Wash the rice like a dhal as described in the introduction (page 16).
2. Soak the rice for about 1 hour in the 390ml (13fl oz) of water.
3. Heat the oil in a pan and add the jeera and rai. Leave to cook for a few seconds.
4. Very carefully add the soaked rice and water, salt, turmeric powder, chilli powder, tomato purée, and peas. If they are added too quickly, the mixture will spit all over the place. Bring the mixture to the boil.
5. Reduce the heat, cover the pan and let it simmer gently for about 20 minutes.
6. Transfer the contents to a serving dish, and serve while hot.

LAMB BIRYANI

Serves 4.

Preparation and cooking time: 1 hr.

This is a mild rice dish, usually served with dhal or a vegetable dish.

170g (6oz) basmati rice
750ml (25fl oz) water
1 small onion, finely chopped
1 green chilli, finely chopped
225g (8oz) boneless lamb, cut into very small 1cm ($^1/_2$ inch) cubes
$^1/_2$ tsp turmeric powder
1 tsp salt
$^1/_2$ tsp chilli powder
2 tsp soy sauce
85g (3oz) frozen peas
85g (3oz) frozen diced carrots

Method
1.   Wash the rice like all dhals, as described on page 16.
2.   In a large pan mix the water, onion, green chilli, lamb, turmeric powder, salt, chilli powder, and soy sauce. Bring to the boil, cover the pan, reduce the heat and let the mixture boil for about 35 minutes.
3.   Add the washed rice, peas and carrots. Bring back to the boil and then reduce the heat again. Cover the pan and simmer gently for about 12 minutes. The rice should look dry.
4.   Transfer the contents to a serving dish and serve hot.

VEGETABLE BIRYANI

Serves 4.

Preparation and cooking time: 40 mins.

If you like rice and are a vegetarian, then vegetable biryani is just the thing for you. It is usually served with fresh salad. For this recipe you need a deep frying pan, or wok, and a liquidizer.

170g (6oz) basmati rice
25g (1oz) fresh garlic, peeled
25g (1oz) fresh ginger, peeled
60ml (2fl oz) cooking oil
3 whole cloves
$^1/_2$ tsp whole jeera (cumin seeds)
$^1/_2$ tsp whole rai (black mustard seeds)
$^1/_4$ tsp hing (asafoetida)
1 large onion, finely chopped
1 tsp tomato purée
110g (4oz) frozen peas
170g (6oz) frozen diced carrots, properly thawed
225g (8oz) frozen cauliflower, properly thawed
1 large potato, finely chopped
$^1/_2$ tsp turmeric powder
1 tsp salt
$^1/_2$ tsp chilli powder
600ml (20fl oz) water

Method

1. Wash the rice, like dhals as described on page 16.
2. Place the garlic and ginger in a liquidizer, and chop finely.
3. Heat the oil to a high temperature in a wok or deep frying pan. Add the cloves, jeera, rai and asafoetida, and cook for a few seconds. Add the chopped onion, and cook until the onion is golden brown.
4. Add the contents of the liquidizer and cook for a further 2 minutes. Add the tomato purée, peas, carrots, cauliflower, potato, turmeric powder, salt and chilli powder. Cook for a further 2 minutes, stirring continuously.
5. Add the water and rice. Bring the mixture to the boil and reduce the heat. Cover the pan and simmer gently for about 15 minutes. The rice should now look dry.
6. Transfer the contents to a serving dish and serve while hot.

PLAIN PAROTHAS

Makes about 16 parothas.

Preparation and cooking time: 40 mins.

Parothas can be served with most curries. They are heavy in calories. They taste nice cold and are therefore useful for picnics, etc. For this recipe you need a large flat frying pan or tava.

900g (2lb) white chapatti flour, sieved
60ml (2fl oz) cooking oil
420ml (14fl oz) water
110g (4oz) chapatti flour, for rolling
480ml (16fl oz) cooking oil, for frying parothas

Method

1. Mix the sieved flour and the 60ml (2fl oz) of cooking oil in a bowl and leave it for a few seconds.

2. Add the water gradually to the above mixture, and continue to mix well, until a medium stiff dough is formed.

3. Divide the above mixture into about 16 roughly equal portions. Sprinkle flour onto a rolling area and roll the balls into discs about 12cm (5 inches) in diameter.

4. Spread a teaspoonful of cooking oil onto the flat rolled chapatti, and sprinkle a little bit of dry flour on top. Fold the chapatti first into halves and then into quarters. Roll out each shape as a triangle, with one curved side, so that the straight sides are about 12cm (5 inches) long.

5. Heat a tava or flat pan and place the rolled parotha on the pan. Leave it for a few seconds. Now turn it over and cook the other side for a few seconds. Turn it back again and cook for a further few seconds.

6. Now spread a teaspoonful of cooking oil on the top of the cooking parotha and turn it over so that the oiled side is underneath. Spread the other side similarly with cooking oil and turn again to cook the second side. Continue cooking until both sides of the parotha are light brown. Remove the parotha from the pan and place it in a dish.

7. Cook all the parothas in this way.

PAROTHAS STUFFED WITH POTATOES

Makes about 16 parothas.

Preparation and cooking time: 1 hr.

Unlike plain parothas, stuffed parothas are often eaten without curries and are cooked for high teas or picnics. Potato stuffed parothas are a favourite with children. For this recipe you need a large flat frying pan or tava.

900g (2lb) potatoes, peeled
1 tsp salt
$^1/_2$ tsp garam masala
$^1/_2$ tsp chilli powder
$^1/_4$ tsp jeera (cumin seeds)
Small amount green dhanyia, (coriander), chopped
900g (2lb) white, chapatti flour, sieved
60ml (2fl oz) cooking oil
420ml (14fl oz) water
110g (4oz) chapatti flour, for rolling
480ml (16fl oz) cooling oil, for frying parothas

Method

1. Boil the potatoes, as if you were making mash.
2. Mash the potatoes and add the salt, garam masala, chilli powder, jeera and the fresh green coriander. Mix everything well.
3. Mix the sieved flour and the 60ml (2fl oz) of cooking oil in a bowl and leave it for a few seconds.
4. Add the water gradually to the above mixture and continue to mix well, until a medium stiff dough is formed.
5. Divide the dough into about 16 roughly equal portions and shape them into balls. Sprinkle flour onto a rolling area and roll the balls into discs about 12cm (5 inches) in diameter.
6. Place two large tablespoonfuls of the spiced mash onto the flat rolled chapatti, and sprinkle a little bit of dry flour on top. Fold the chapatti into a ball so that the mash is completely covered by the dough. Roll out the balls again into discs about 17cm (7 inches) in diameter.
7. Heat a tava or flat pan to a high temperature and place the rolled parotha on the pan. Leave it for a few seconds. Now turn it over and cook the other side for a few seconds. Turn it back again and cook for a further few seconds.
8. Now spread a teaspoonful of cooking oil on the top of the cooking parotha and turn it over so that the oiled side is underneath. Spread the other side similarly with the cooking oil and turn again to cook the second side. Continue cooking until both sides of the parotha are light brown. Remove the parotha from the pan and place it in a dish.
9. Cook all the parothas in this way.

PAROTHAS STUFFED WITH CAULIFLOWER

Makes about 8 parothas.

Preparation and cooking time: 1 hr.

Stuffed parothas do not need curries and they are often cooked for high teas or picnics. Cauliflower stuffed parothas are very different and sometimes served for breakfast, in the northern parts of India. For this recipe you need a large flat frying pan or tava and a grater.

450g (1lb) cauliflower
$^1/_2$ tsp salt
$^1/_2$ tsp garam masala
$^1/_2$ tsp chilli powder
450g (1lb) white chapatti flour, sieved
30ml (1fl oz) cooking oil
210ml (7fl oz) water
110g (4oz) chapatti flour, for rolling
240ml (8fl oz) cooking oil, for frying parothas

Method

1. Cut and wash the cauliflower and then grate it.

2. Mix the cauliflower, salt, garam masala and the chilli powder. After mixing, squeeze out all the water from the grated spiced cauliflower.

3. Mix the sieved flour and the 30ml (1fl oz) of cooking oil in a bowl and leave it for a few seconds.

4. Add the water gradually, to the above mixture and continue to mix well, until a medium stiff dough is formed. Leave the dough in a cool place for about 30 minutes.

5. Divide the dough into about 8 roughly equal portions and shape them into balls. Sprinkle flour onto a rolling area and roll the balls into discs about 15cm (6 inches) in diameter.

6. Place two tablespoonfuls of spiced cauliflower onto the flat rolled chapatti, and sprinkle a little bit of dry flour on top. Fold the chapatti into a ball in such a way that the cauliflower is completely covered by the dough. Roll out the balls again into discs, about 17cm (7 inches) in diameter.

7. Heat a tava or flat pan to a high temperature and place the rolled parotha on the pan. Leave it for a few seconds. Now turn it over and cook the other side for a few seconds. Turn it over again and cook for a further few seconds.

8. Now spread a teaspoonful of cooking oil on top of the cooking parotha and turn it over so that the oiled side is underneath. Spread the other side similarly with cooking oil and turn again to cook the second side. Continue cooking until both sides of the parotha are light brown. Remove the parotha from the pan and place it in a dish.

9. Cook all the parothas in this way.

PURIS

Makes about 25 puris.

Preparation and cooking time: 50 mins.

Puris are very similar to chapattis but are deep fried. This deep frying process gives them a slightly different taste from chapattis. For this recipe you need a deep frying pan or wok.

450g (1lb) white chapatti flour, sieved
30ml (1fl oz) cooking oil
210ml (7fl oz) water
55g (2oz) chapatti flour, for rolling
1200ml (40fl oz) cooking oil, for deep frying

Method
1. Place the sieved flour in the bowl and add the 30ml (1fl oz) cooking oil. Mix together for a few seconds.
2. Add the water gradually, and continue to mix, until a medium soft dough is formed which can be kneaded.
3. Divide the mixture into about 25 balls. Sprinkle flour on the rolling area and roll each ball flat into a round shape about 12cm (5 inches) in diameter.
4. Heat the oil to a high temperature in a deep frying pan or wok. Once the oil is hot keep it at a steady temperature, at about medium heat. Place the rolled puri in the oil and fry for about 20 seconds. Now turn and fry the other side for about the same time. The puri should turn golden brown. If the colour changes to golden brown very quickly, then lower the heat.
5. You may find it easier to roll out all the puris first, lay them out separately, and then deep fry them individually. Once you get used to the process then both rolling and frying can be done concurrently.
6. Serve the puris hot.

LASSI

Serves 4.

Preparation and cooking time: 35 mins.

This is a yoghurt drink often served at meals. It may be served sweet or salty dependent on personal preference. For this recipe you need a whisk.

250ml (8fl oz) natural fresh yoghurt
300ml (10fl oz) water
$^1/_2$ tsp salt or 1 tsp sugar

Method
1. Mix the yoghurt, water and salt (or sugar) in a large jug and whisk together for approximately 5 minutes.
2. Leave the mixture called lassi, to cool in the fridge for about 30 minutes.
3. Serve cold.

SAFFRON ALMOND MILK

Serves 4.

Preparation and cooking time: 30 mins.

This is sometimes served at night, just before going to bed. Try it instead of some other night time drink.

1200ml (40fl oz) milk
A pinch of saffron
10g (¹/₂oz) almonds, finely chopped

Method
1. In a large pan, mix the milk and the saffron. Bring the milk to the boil, lower the heat and let the milk simmer very gently for about 20 minutes.
2. Add the almonds and simmer for a further 5 minutes. Serve hot or cold. Sugar may be added, dependent on taste.

8
SWEETS

DRY SWEET VERMICELLI

Serves 4.

Preparation and cooking time: 40 mins.

This is a sweet dish served as a dessert. It is not served in restaurants and therefore well worth trying at home.

85g (3oz) sugar
450ml (15fl oz) water
170g (6oz) vermicelli
55g (2oz) ghee
$^1/_2$ tsp ground cardamom
$^1/_2$ tsp nutmeg
25g (1oz) almonds, finely chopped

Method
1. Mix the sugar and water and bring the mixture to the boil.
2. Cook the vermicelli and ghee together, on a very low heat, stirring continuously, until the vermicelli turns golden brown. This usually takes about 15 to 20 minutes.
3. Add the sugar syrup, cardamom and nutmeg and stir well. Bring the mixture to the boil, reduce the heat and simmer gently until the water has evaporated. This will usually take about 15 minutes.
4. Transfer the contents to a serving dish and garnish with almonds. Serve while hot.

KHEER
(Rice pudding)

Serves 4.

Preparation and cooking time: 1 hr.

This is a sweet dish, similar to the traditional English rice pudding. It is usually served as a dessert and can be served hot or cold dependent on choice.

110g (4oz) patna rice, or long grain white rice
300ml (10fl oz) water
900ml (30fl oz) milk
A pinch of saffron
85g (3oz) sugar
$^1/_4$ tsp ground cardamom
$^1/_4$ tsp ground nutmeg
25g (1oz) almonds, finely chopped
25g (1oz) pistachios, finely chopped

Method
1. Wash the rice and add the 300ml (10fl oz) of water.
2. Bring the water to the boil.
3. Reduce the heat, cover the pan and simmer gently for about 8 minutes, until the water has evaporated. Add the milk and saffron. Bring it to the boil. Reduce the heat. If the mixture starts sticking to the bottom of the pot, lower the heat further. Simmer gently for about 30 minutes, stirring every 5 to 7 minutes.
4. Add sugar and simmer gently for a further 15 minutes, stirring every 5 to 7 minutes.
5. Switch off the heat. Place the cooked rice pudding in a serving dish.
6. Garnish with the ground cardamom, nutmeg, chopped almonds and pistachios.

GULAB JAMAN

Makes about 30 gulab jaman.

Preparation and cooking time: 1 hr 20 mins.

This is a very sweet dish, often served as a dessert after a hot curry. It can also be served at parties or with high tea. It may be served hot or cold dependent on personal preference. For this recipe you need a deep frying pan or wok.

450g (1lb) sugar
600ml (20fl oz) water
225g (8oz) gulab jaman powder or milk powder
25g (1oz) self raising flour
25g (1oz) plain flour
$^{1}/_{4}$ tsp ground cardamom
$^{1}/_{4}$ tsp ground nutmeg
55g (2oz) melted butter
A pinch of saffron or 5 to 7 drops yellow food colouring
10g ($^{1}/_{2}$oz) fine desiccated coconut
120ml (4fl oz) milk
600ml (20fl oz) cooking oil, for frying

Method

1. Place the sugar in a pan, add the water and bring it to the boil. Lower the heat and simmer gently for about 5 minutes.

2. Place the gulab jaman powder (or milk powder) in a mixing bowl. Add the self raising flour, plain flour, ground cardamom, nutmeg, melted butter, saffron (or food colouring) and coconut. Mix well, adding the milk gradually; thus turning the mixture into a soft dough. Divide the dough into about 30 equal parts and shape each into a smooth round ball.

3. Heat the oil in a wok or deep frying pan to a temperature so that when a crumb of bread is thrown into the oil, it browns within 15 seconds. Now reduce the heat to a simmer. Place the gulab jaman, four at a time, in the wok and fry until the balls turn dark brown. Remove them from the oil and place them on a kitchen towel.

4. After all the gulab jaman have been fried, transfer the sugar syrup to a serving dish and add the gulab jaman. Leave the gulab jaman soaking in the syrup for about 30 minutes before serving.

5. If you like them cold then leave the gulab jaman in the syrup, for about 30 minutes in the fridge. If you like them hot then heat the syrup and the gulab jaman for about 10 minutes.

BESAN BARFI
(Gram flour fudge)

Serves 4.

Preparation and cooking time: 4 hrs 40 mins.

This is another dessert dish. It is not as sweet as gulab jaman and is
served cold. It tastes very much like fudge and can be stored for up
to 1 week after cooking. It can also be served at high teas or picnics.
For this recipe you need a deep frying pan or wok.

110g (4oz) sugar
120ml (4fl oz) water
225g (8oz) gram flour
110g (4oz) ghee
110g (4oz) gulab jaman powder or milk powder
5 drops yellow food colouring or a pinch of yellow food colouring
    powder
1/4 tsp ground nutmeg
1/4 tsp ground cardamom
25g (1oz) almonds, finely chopped

Method

1. Place the sugar and water in a pan and bring the mixture to the boil. Simmer gently for about 8 or 9 minutes.

2. Sieve the gram flour into a wok or deep frying pan and add the ghee. Cook the mixture on a very low heat, stirring continuously, until the flour is golden brown.

3. Add the gulab jaman powder (or milk powder) and cook for another 2 minutes, stirring continuously.

4. Now add the sugar syrup. Stir continuously over a very low heat until the mixture is thick and sticky, very much like jam.

5. Remove the mixture from the heat, add the colouring, nutmeg and cardamom powder and mix well. Place the mixture in a greased tray. Garnish with the almonds and leave it to cool down. While the mixture is still warm, cut it completely through, into cubes like fudge. Leave it to set for a further 4 hours. Separate the cubes.

6. This dessert is served cold.

CARROT HALVA
(A sweet carrot dessert)

Serves 4.

Preparation and cooking time: 2 hrs 40 mins.

This is a sweet and tasty carrot dish. It can be served hot or cold and this makes it more flexible.

340g (12oz) carrots
90ml (3fl oz) water
$1/4$ tsp ground cardamom or 3 whole cardamoms, crushed
A pinch of saffron
180ml (6fl oz) milk
55g (2oz) sugar
1 tsp melted unsalted butter or ghee
25g (1oz) almonds (skinless)

Method
1. Peel, and then grate the carrots.
2. Mix the grated carrots, water, cardamom and saffron in a large pan. Bring the water to the boil and then lower the heat. Cover the pan, and simmer gently for about 1 hour, stirring every 10 to 15 minutes.
3. Add the milk and sugar and simmer for a further 1 hour on a low heat.
4. Add the butter or ghee, and evaporate the milk on a gentle heat. This usually takes about 15 minutes, and at the end you are left with very little liquid in the carrots.
5. Transfer the contents to a serving dish and decorate with the almonds. Serve either hot or cold.

KULFI
(Indian ice cream)

Serves 4.

Preparation and cooking time: 5 hrs 30 mins.

Kulfi is the Indian version of ice cream. It is very sweet and like most Indian desserts very heavy in calories. Most Indian children love kulfi.

600ml (20fl oz) full cream milk
300ml (10fl oz) condensed milk
55g (2oz) skinless almonds, finely chopped
25g (1oz) unsalted pistachio nuts, shells removed, finely chopped
85g (3oz) sugar

Method
1. Mix all the ingredients in a large pan, and bring the mixture to the boil.
2. Lower the heat, and let the mixture simmer for about one and a half hours, stirring every 30 minutes.
3. Transfer the mixture to an ice cube tray. Let it cool and then leave it to set, in a freezer, or the freezer compartment of a fridge for about 3 hours.
4. When you are ready to serve, remove the tray from the freezer, separate the cubes and serve in small fruit bowls.

SEMOLINA HALVA

Serves 4.

Preparation and cooking time: 45 mins.

Semolina halva is usually served in Sikh and Hindu temples. It is popular with vegetarians. It is a very sweet dessert and contains a large amount of fat.

420ml (14fl oz) water
110g (4oz) sugar
¹/₄ tsp ground cardamom
140g (5oz) butter
110g (4oz) semolina

Method
1. Mix the water, sugar and cardamom and bring the mixture to the boil. Switch off heat.
2. In a large saucepan melt the butter. Lower the heat, and add the semolina. Stir continuously and cook until the semolina turns golden brown. This will usually take about 9 to 10 minutes.
3. Now add the water and sugar mixture, stirring continuously. Do this carefully, because, when first poured, the water will froth and may spit out of the pot. Make sure that you stir continuously, otherwise the mixture will become lumpy.
4. Increase the heat and bring the mixture to the boil. Lower the heat and cook for about a further 4 minutes stirring continuously. The mixture will be very thick and pasty.
5. Transfer the contents to a serving bowl and serve hot.

SAFFRON APPLE
AND ALMOND PUDDING

Serves 4.

Preparation and cooking time: 20 mins.

If you like apples then this dish is worth a try. It can be served with hot or cold custard, or cream.

450g (1lb) eating apples
120ml (4fl oz) water
110g (4oz) sugar
A pinch of saffron
2 tsp cornflour mixed with 2 tsp water
110g (4oz) almonds, finely chopped

Method
1   Peel the apples and remove the cores. Cut the apples into chip-shaped pieces.
2   Mix the apples, water, sugar and saffron in a pan and bring to the boil. Lower the heat, cover the pan and let the apples simmer for about 5 minutes.
3   Add the cornflour mixed with the water, mix well and let the mixture simmer for a further 2 or 3 minutes.
4   Transfer the contents to a serving dish and garnish with the almonds. Serve hot or cold (depending on taste) with cream or custard.

SAFFRON APPLE AND ALMOND PUDDING

APPENDIX

SPICE NAMES

It is always cheaper to buy spices in larger packs rather than in small 55g (2oz) cartons. Most Indian spices are cheaper at Indian grocery shops and, if you know the Indian names, it makes it that much easier. So for the difficult spices here are the Indian names and their equivalent English names.

INDIAN NAME	ENGLISH NAME
Adhrak or Adhu	Ginger
Anardana	Pomegranate seeds
Atta	Chapatti flour
Badam	Almonds
Besan or Chana na loth	Gram flour
Dalchini	Cinnamon sticks
Dhanyia	Coriander
Haldi	Turmeric powder
Hing	Asafoetida
Jaifal	Nutmeg, whole
Jeera	Cumin seeds
Kala chana or Kale chole	Gram kichererbsen
Kali mirch sabat or Marri	Whole black peppercorns
Lachi or Alchee	Cardamoms
Lasan	Garlic
Methi	Fenugreek
Rai	Black mustard seeds
Soonf or Variari	Fennel seeds
Toovar or Har har di dahl	Hushed pigeon peas
Urad or Mahan di dahl	Black matape
White Chana or Chite chole	Chick peas

ENGLISH NAME	INDIAN NAME
Almonds	Badam
Asafoetida	Hing
Black matape	Urad or Mahan di dah
Black mustard seeds	Rai
Cardamoms	Lachi or Alchee
Chapatti flour	Atta
Chick peas	White chana or Chite chole
Cinnamon sticks	Dalchini
Coriander	Dhanyia
Cumin seeds	Jeera
Fennel seeds	Soonf or Variari
Fenugreek	Methi
Garlic	Lasan
Ginger	Adhrak or Adhu
Gram flour	Besan or Chana na loth
Gram kichererbsen	Kale chana or Kale chole
Hushed pigeon peas	Toovar or Har har di dahl
Nutmeg, whole	Jaifal
Pomegranate seeds	Anardana
Turmeric powder	Haldi
Whole black peppercorns	Kali mirch sabat or Marri

INDEX